Oracle JET for Developers

Implement client-side JavaScript efficiently for enterprise
Oracle applications

Raja Malleswara Rao Pattamsetti

BIRMINGHAM - MUMBAI

Oracle JET for Developers

First published: December 2017

Production reference: 1061217

Published by Packt Publishing Ltd.
Livery Place
35 Livery Street
Birmingham
B3 2PB, UK.

ISBN 978-1-78728-474-6

www.packtpub.com

Credits

Author
Raja Malleswara Rao Pattamsetti

Reviewer
Bogunuva Mohanram Balachandar

Commissioning Editor
Amarabha Banerjee

Acquisition Editor
Denim Pinto

Content Development Editor
Vikas Tiwari

Technical Editor
Subhalaxmi Nadar

Copy Editor
Safis Editing

Project Coordinator
Ulhas Kambali

Proofreader
Safis Editing

Indexer
Pratik Shirodkar

Graphics
Jason Monteiro

Production Coordinator
Nilesh Mohite

About the Author

Raja Malleswara Rao Pattamsetti is a Java architect, focusing on enterprise architecture and the development of applications with web, Java, and related technologies on the cloud. He is a certified Java and web components developer with deep expertise in building enterprise applications using diverse frameworks and methodologies. He is an active participant in technical forums, groups, and conferences. He has worked with several Fortune 500 organizations and is passionate about learning new technologies and their developments. He has also authored the books, *Distributed Computing in Java 9* and *Spring Batch Essentials* by Packt.

I would like to thank my family and friends for their love and support, especially my wife, Bhargavi, for encouraging me through this stint.
I should thank my reviewers, for their valuable suggestions in improving the quality of this book, and my colleagues and the web community, for sharing great thoughts, which helped me a lot in keeping myself updated.

About the Reviewer

Bogunuva Mohanram Balachandar is a senior architect with a leading American multinational corporation listed in NASDAQ-100 that provides digital, technology, consulting, and operations services. He has over 16 years of IT industry experience in software design and development. Prior to joining his current employer, he has worked with IBM, Accenture, and Wipro. He has extensive experience in the design and development of multiple Enterprise Application Integration projects using various tools and technologies, such as Oracle SOA Suite, Oracle Service Bus, Oracle AIA, IBM WebSphere Process Server, web services, RESTful services, **Business Process Execution Language** (**BPEL**), IBM WebSphere MQ, TIBCO EMS, Java, JMS, and Spring integration. He is certified in SOA, web services, and cloud technologies from IBM and Oracle.

I would like to thank the Packt team for giving me this opportunity. I would also like to thank my wife, Lakshmi, for taking care of all the home affairs, requiring minimal intervention from my end, and helping me to secure time for reviewing this book.

www.PacktPub.com

For support files and downloads related to your book, please visit www.PacktPub.com.

Did you know that Packt offers eBook versions of every book published, with PDF and ePub files available? You can upgrade to the eBook version at www.PacktPub.com and as a print book customer, you are entitled to a discount on the eBook copy. Get in touch with us at service@packtpub.com for more details.

At www.PacktPub.com, you can also read a collection of free technical articles, sign up for a range of free newsletters and receive exclusive discounts and offers on Packt books and eBooks.

https://www.packtpub.com/mapt

Get the most in-demand software skills with Mapt. Mapt gives you full access to all Packt books and video courses, as well as industry-leading tools to help you plan your personal development and advance your career.

Why subscribe?

- Fully searchable across every book published by Packt
- Copy and paste, print, and bookmark content
- On demand and accessible via a web browser

Customer Feedback

Thanks for purchasing this Packt book. At Packt, quality is at the heart of our editorial process. To help us improve, please leave us an honest review on this book's Amazon page at https://www.amazon.com/dp/1787284743.

If you'd like to join our team of regular reviewers, you can email us at customerreviews@packtpub.com. We award our regular reviewers with free eBooks and videos in exchange for their valuable feedback. Help us be relentless in improving our products!

Table of Contents

Preface

In real-world enterprise application design and development, multiple aspects need to be considered, starting from building a simple drop-down list to developing platform-independent features such as accessibility or UI consistency, which are left unattended more often than not. Oracle JavaScript Extension Toolkit (JET) gives you the set of important building blocks needed for your application, and it doesn't forget about making your application mature, in terms of internationalization, localization, and multiplatform development.

While we describe each of the concepts with a detailed explanation and handy diagrams that aptly represent the components and developer actions, we also bring appropriate examples and code snippets to help you understand how they can be implemented with the help of Oracle JET.

There are numerous improvements to the Oracle JET concepts and additional features that enable support for the development of web applications with Oracle JET. We'll discuss each of the Oracle JET concepts, along with improvements and their implementation in, separate chapters; these concepts have helped the field of web development advance further over the last few decades. This should cover the design thoughts and security aspects as well, which we believe lets you concentrate on each specific topic and understand it a step further with the right combination of explanations, diagrams, and code snippets.

This book took about 6 months for me to write and it was a great journey. The design and development experiences with multiple enterprise applications on cloud portfolio and webpack systems, along with the support of solution architecture teams, helped me go through the on-ground challenges and improve the design standpoint of the web interface. There are many places where I start talking about the project development life cycle, Agile, TDD and BDD, and the importance of rapid development and automated tests on UI development before the solution implementation specifics. Also, care has been taken to help you with the explanation of the concepts in such a way that you'll feel like you're participating in a detailed technical conversation.

Most of the concepts are imbued with an everlasting perception of reusability and thorough engineering, and I believe some parts of this will remain with you as useful techniques to reuse in your application development.

Finally, while I've made sure to complement every chapter with plenty of illustrations to get the desired output, I think it is paramount for you to review each concept and practice it, so you learn and build your confidence of working with such systems.

Have fun building great things!

What this book covers

Chapter 1, *Getting Started with Oracle JET*, gets you started with using Oracle JET, bootstrapping the project, and understanding the project's base architecture.

Chapter 2, *Oracle Alta UI*, explores the different ways of using the UI framework, Alta, in Oracle JET.

Chapter 3, *Tools Integration*, explains how to integrate Oracle JET into your build pipeline. The most popular build tools are covered in this chapter.

Chapter 4, *Knockout JS*, introduces and explores Knockout, the library behind OJ. It also covers best practices around it.

Chapter 5, *Oracle JET Components – Form Elements, Controls, and Data Collections*, covers the handling of components related to collections, controls, and forms.

Chapter 6, *Oracle JET Components – Layouts, Navigation, and Visualizations*, discusses the components related to layouts, navigation, and graph visualizations.

Chapter 7, *Framework*, explains the application part of an OJ project. The chapter is divided into two subsections covering a wide spectrum of concepts, from component validations to routing and tests.

Chapter 8, *Hybrid Mobile Application Development* explains how a multiplatform application can be set up and developed.

Chapter 9, *Testing and Debugging*, explores the testing and debugging of Oracle JET applications.

Chapter 10, *Security and Version Migration*, examines different security issues and constraints associated with web applications, what to look for when the version changes, and what's to come in the next Oracle JET versions.

What you need for this book

To follow along with this book, you'll need a computer with an internet connection. You can choose to work online on a JSFiddle kind of cloud web environment to practice the examples. I recommend that you have the NetBeans IDE with Grunt, Oracle JET, and the HTML5 extension along with a Chrome browser containing the NetBeans runner.

Who this book is for

This book has been tested on people who have a decent programming knowledge of web applications with basic HTML, CSS, and JavaScript, and who wanted to venture into learning a framework that will help them build features on top of the base components. They picked up with practice and by the end of the book, they gained a thorough knowledge of Oracle JET and its design aspects. Through this book, you will learn some tricks and tips that you didn't know about and be given wise suggestions that will help you along the way.

This book, if followed from cover to cover, will turn you into a proficient web interface expert. On the other hand, if you already are, it provides a good reference for many different features and techniques that may come in handy from time to time. Finally, this book is also a valid migration guide if you have already experimented with Oracle JET concepts and felt overwhelmed by the change.

Conventions

In this book, you will find a number of text styles that distinguish between different kinds of information. Here are some examples of these styles and an explanation of their meaning. Code words in text, database table names, folder names, filenames, file extensions, pathnames, dummy URLs, user input, and Twitter handles are shown as follows: "Similarly, we have added another `markedEmployee`."

A block of code is set as follows:

```
<td data-bind='text: name'></td>
```

Any command-line input or output is written as follows:

```
npm -g install yo grunt-cli
```

New terms and **important words** are shown in bold. Words that you see on the screen, for example, in menus or dialog boxes, appear in the text like this: "Click on the **Install** button, which should install Node.js, along with the npm package manager, on your computer."

Warnings or important notes appear like this.

Tips and tricks appear like this.

Reader feedback

Feedback from our readers is always welcome. Let us know what you think about this book-what you liked or disliked. Reader feedback is important for us as it helps us develop titles that you will really get the most out of. To send us general feedback, simply email feedback@packtpub.com, and mention the book's title in the subject of your message. If there is a topic that you have expertise in and you are interested in either writing or contributing to a book, see our author guide at www.packtpub.com/authors.

Customer support

Now that you are the proud owner of a Packt book, we have a number of things to help you to get the most from your purchase.

Downloading the example code

You can download the example code files for this book from your account at http://www.packtpub.com. If you purchased this book elsewhere, you can visit http://www.packtpub.com/support and register to have the files emailed directly to you. You can download the code files by following these steps:

1. Log in or register to our website using your email address and password.
2. Hover the mouse pointer on the **SUPPORT** tab at the top.
3. Click on **Code Downloads & Errata**.
4. Enter the name of the book in the **Search** box.
5. Select the book for which you're looking to download the code files.

6. Choose from the drop-down menu where you purchased this book from.
7. Click on **Code Download**.

Once the file is downloaded, please make sure that you unzip or extract the folder using the latest version of:

- WinRAR / 7-Zip for Windows
- Zipeg / iZip / UnRarX for Mac
- 7-Zip / PeaZip for Linux

The code bundle for the book is also hosted on GitHub at `https://github.com/PacktPublishing/Oracle-JET-for-Developers`. We also have other code bundles from our rich catalog of books and videos available at `https://github.com/PacktPublishing/`. Check them out!

Downloading the color images of this book

We also provide you with a PDF file that has color images of the screenshots/diagrams used in this book. The color images will help you better understand the changes in the output. You can download this file from `http://www.packtpub.com/sites/default/files/downloads/OracleJETforDevelopers_ColorImages.pdf`.

Errata

Although we have taken every care to ensure the accuracy of our content, mistakes do happen. If you find a mistake in one of our books-maybe a mistake in the text or the code-we would be grateful if you could report this to us. By doing so, you can save other readers from frustration and help us improve subsequent versions of this book. If you find any errata, please report them by visiting `http://www.packtpub.com/submit-errata`, selecting your book, clicking on the **Errata Submission Form** link, and entering the details of your errata. Once your errata are verified, your submission will be accepted and the errata will be uploaded to our website or added to any list of existing errata under the Errata section of that title. To view the previously submitted errata, go to `https://www.packtpub.com/books/content/support` and enter the name of the book in the search field. The required information will appear under the **Errata** section.

Piracy

Piracy of copyrighted material on the internet is an ongoing problem across all media. At Packt, we take the protection of our copyright and licenses very seriously. If you come across any illegal copies of our works in any form on the internet, please provide us with the location address or website name immediately so that we can pursue a remedy. Please contact us at `copyright@packtpub.com` with a link to the suspected pirated material. We appreciate your help in protecting our authors and our ability to bring you valuable content.

Questions

If you have a problem with any aspect of this book, you can contact us at `questions@packtpub.com`, and we will do our best to address the problem.

1
Getting Started with Oracle JET

Rapid application development is the trend of building web applications today with the evolution of web 2.0 and the web frameworks. They are no more just represent the View portion of the MVC architecture, but also cover the responsibility of MVC architecture on the application interface (client-side MVC). This has become a reality with the growth of a number of web frameworks over the last decade. This has motivated organizations like Google and Facebook to develop frameworks such as Angular JS and React JS, which are ready to serve cloud application architecture. The Oracle Corporation observed the trend and appraised the future needs of web applications and developed a simple but efficient web framework by integrating Oracle and open source JavaScript libraries.

In this chapter we will cover:

- Getting started with Oracle JET
- How to bootstrap your first Oracle JET project
- Setting up npm and Node.js
- Installing Yeoman and Grunt
- Installing Oracle JET generator
- Creating a project using the command line
- Running a project with Grunt
- Managing and running the project using the NetBeans IDE

Getting started with Oracle JET

Oracle **JavaScript Extension Toolkit** (**JET**) is an engineered toolkit containing the Oracle and open source JavaScript libraries. It supports the **Model-View-ViewModel** (**MVVM**) architecture, which allows the model to represent the application data, the view for the presentation, and the ViewModel to help manage the application state and expose data from the model to the view. The framework empowers the application developers by providing an open source modular toolkit developed using the recent JavaScript, HTML5, and CSS3 architecture principles. Oracle JET helps developers build both web-based and hybrid (mobile) applications that can easily integrate with other server-side applications and products running on cloud environments as well. It uses the trendy Oracle Alta UI for adding the application and to easily match your business context.

The following diagram represents the Oracle JET framework alignment in MVVM design:

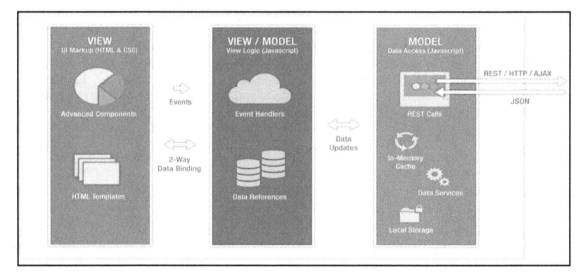

Oracle JET features

The following are the set of features provided by the Oracle JET framework:

- Comprehensive toolkit for web development
- Embeds the widely known open source frameworks
- Single-Page Application development support with template-based architecture and a powerful routing system

- Built-in support for accessibility
- Messaging and event services for both the model and view layer
- Great support for internationalization, with more than 28 languages and 180 locales
- Set of efficient and useful UI components with a validation framework
- Two-way binding at its best
- Better resource organization
- Built-in support for mobile application development
- Caching to support efficient pagination
- Support for REST service invocation
- Integrated authorization using the OAuth 2.0 data model for REST services

 Single-Page Applications (**SPAs**) are web apps that load a single HTML page and dynamically update that page as the user interacts with the app. SPAs use AJAX and HTML5 to create fluid and responsive web apps without constant page reloads.

Oracle JET makes use of the following popular open source libraries along with JET components:

- **jQuery**: JavaScript library with a range of useful utilities for REST, AJAX, animations, and JSON handling
- **jQuery UI**: Helps in wrapping the Oracle JET components as robust UI components
- **Knockout JS**: Provides two-way data binding support
- **RequireJS**: Provides modularity and lazy loading of the resources via **Asynchronous Module Definition** (**AMD**)
- **Syntactically Awesome Style Sheets** (**SASS**): Extends CSS3 to enable nested rules, inline imports, and mixins
- **Apache Cordova**: For hybrid (mobile) application development
- **Oracle Alta UI**: The UI design system for trendy interface design

Bootstrapping your first Oracle JET project

Generating your first Oracle JET project, managing it using an IDE, and running it on your computer is way easier with a modern set of tools and techniques such as Node.js, npm, Yeoman, and Grunt.

All this can be achieved using the standard mechanism including the following steps:

You can also use other techniques, such as generating the project using IDE plugins or downloading the ZIP version of the templates and importing them into projects. ZIP versions are available for download at http://www.oracle.com/technetwork/developer-tools/jet/downloads/index.html.

Setting up npm and Node.js

Before setting up npm and Node.js, let us understand these terminologies and how they help us in application development. Node.js is a JavaScript runtime environment built on Chrome's V8 JavaScript engine. Node.js uses an event-driven, non-blocking I/O model that makes it lightweight and efficient. npm from Node.js is the package manager for JavaScript which helps in discovering the packages of reusable code and assembles them in powerful new ways. By using npm, you can install, share, and distribute your code easily and manage the project dependencies wisely. Node.js installation comes with npm and can be downloaded and installed from its home page.

We used the latest stable version available (v6.11.1 LTS) for the setup, as shown in the following steps:

1. Download Node.js, installable from its home page (https://nodejs.org/en/).
2. Run the installable, which starts up with the following interface:

3. Click **Next** and accept the terms in the following interface:

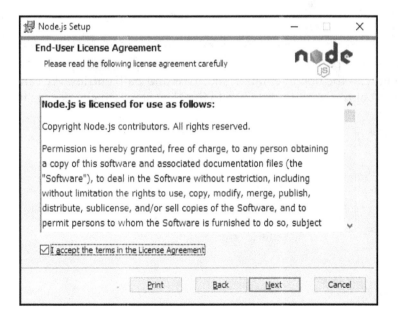

4. Choose the installation directory. I am happy with the default directory provided and continue to the **Next** step, as follows:

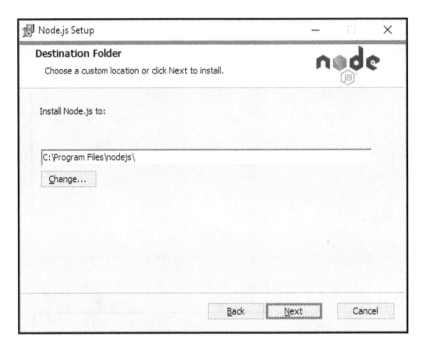

5. The next step gives us the Node.js runtime engine and npm package manager along with the documentation shortcuts and path entries. We can leave the default options selected and go to the **Next** step, which takes us to the final step:

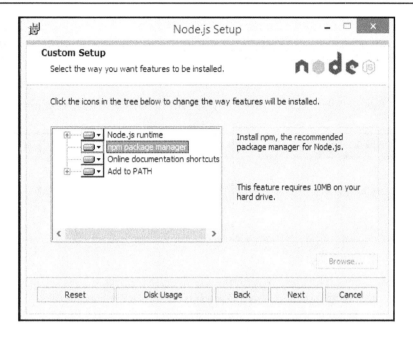

6. Click on the **Install** button, which should install Node.js, along with the npm package manager, on your computer:

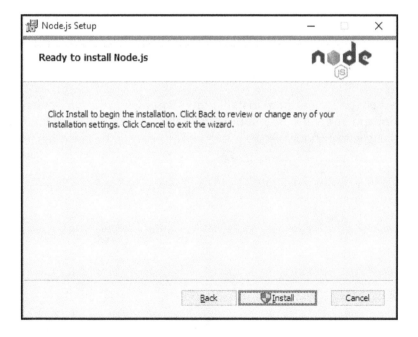

Please be advised that neither the Node.js nor the npm have GUI. They are only accessible through the command line interface, hence you would need to run the commands on the command line.

7. Once the installation is complete, you should see the success status as follows:

8. Once the Node.js and npm installation is complete, you can open the command prompt and verify the installation and version using the commands shown in the following screenshot:

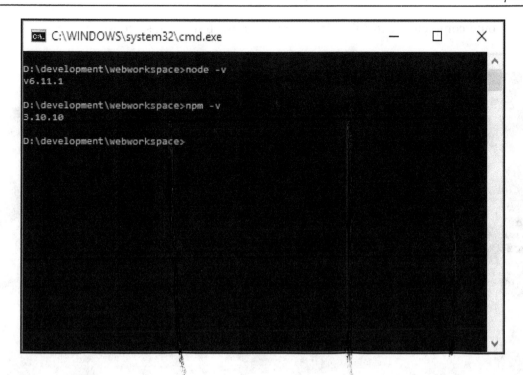

Installing Yeoman and Grunt

Yeoman is the scaffolding tool for web applications, and easily kick starts your new web project development, ensuring the best practices are covered. This means that you don't have to go through the initial project setup tasks you would normally go through to get started; instead, get ready to use application structures along with modular architecture.

Grunt is a JavaScript task runner, a tool used to automatically perform frequent tasks such as minification, compilation, unit testing, linting (the process of running a program that will analyze code for potential errors), and so on. It uses a command-line interface to run custom tasks defined in a file (known as a Gruntfile). Grunt helps in automating the tedious non-functional activities such as minimization, compilation, unit testing, and linting. It's much easier than the method we have been using for years.

We can install them together using the following command:

```
npm -g install yo grunt-cli
```

This should complete the installation, as shown in the following screenshot:

```
C:\WINDOWS\system32\cmd.exe                                                               —  □  ×

D:\development\webworkspace>npm -g install yo grunt-cli
C:\Users\DELL\AppData\Roaming\npm\grunt -> C:\Users\DELL\AppData\Roaming\npm\node_modules\grunt-cli\bin\grunt
C:\Users\DELL\AppData\Roaming\npm\yo-complete -> C:\Users\DELL\AppData\Roaming\npm\node_modules\yo\lib\completion\index.js
C:\Users\DELL\AppData\Roaming\npm\yo -> C:\Users\DELL\AppData\Roaming\npm\node_modules\yo\lib\cli.js

> yo@2.0.0 postinstall C:\Users\DELL\AppData\Roaming\npm\node_modules\yo
> yodoctor

Yeoman Doctor
Running sanity checks on your system

√ Global configuration file is valid
√ NODE_PATH matches the npm root
√ Node.js version
√ No .bowerrc file in home directory
√ No .yo-rc.json file in home directory
√ npm version

Everything looks all right!
C:\Users\DELL\AppData\Roaming\npm
+-- grunt-cli@1.2.0
| +-- findup-sync@0.3.0
| | `-- glob@5.0.15
| |   +-- inflight@1.0.6
| |   | `-- wrappy@1.0.2
| |   +-- inherits@2.0.3
| |   +-- minimatch@3.0.4
| |   | `-- brace-expansion@1.1.8
| |   |   +-- balanced-match@1.0.0
| |   |   `-- concat-map@0.0.1
| |   +-- once@1.4.0
| |   `-- path-is-absolute@1.0.1
| +-- grunt-known-options@1.1.0
| +-- nopt@3.0.6
| | `-- abbrev@1.1.0
| `-- resolve@1.1.7
`-- yo@2.0.0
  `-- inquirer@3.2.0
    `-- string-width@2.1.1

D:\development\webworkspace>_
```

Installing Oracle JET generator

Oracle JET generator is a Yeoman generator for Oracle JET maintained by the Oracle Corporation. It helps us rapidly perform the project setup for a web application or hybrid mobile application on Android, iOS, or Windows.

It can be installed using the following command:

```
npm -g install generator-oraclejet
```

This should complete the installation, as shown in the following screenshot:

Creating a project using the command line

Once Node.js, npm, Yeoman, Grunt, and the Oracle JET Yeoman generator are installed, we shall create a new project using the `oraclejet` command. The beauty of this command is that it generates the project with the name given by the readily available project, which is already created and stored in the node library with the code generator. The following are the steps involved in creating the project with this command:

1. The `oraclejet` Yeoman command with the project name parameter creates the project with the name provided:

    ```
    yo oraclejet <project name> --template=navdrawer
    ```

2. We are using the project name `OracleJETSample`, which should complete the project creation, as shown in the following screenshot:

```
C:\WINDOWS\system32\cmd.exe                                          —    □    ×

D:\development\netbeansworkspace>yo oraclejet OracleJETSample --template=navdrawer
Processing template... navdrawer
Oracle JET: Your app structure is generated. Continuing with library install...
Performing npm install may take a bit...
Invoking npm install
npm WARN prefer global coffee-script@1.10.0 should be installed with -g
OracleJETSample@1.0.0 D:\development\netbeansworkspace\OracleJETSample
+-- grunt@1.0.1
| +-- coffee-script@1.10.0
| +-- dateformat@1.0.12
| | +-- get-stdin@4.0.1
| | `-- meow@3.7.0
| |   +-- camelcase-keys@2.1.0
| |   | `-- camelcase@2.1.1
| |   +-- decamelize@1.2.0
| |   +-- loud-rejection@1.6.0
| |   | +-- currently-unhandled@0.4.1
| |   | | `-- array-find-index@1.0.2
| |   | `-- signal-exit@3.0.2
| |   +-- map-obj@1.0.1
| |   +-- minimist@1.2.0
| |   +-- normalize-package-data@2.4.0
| |   | +-- hosted-git-info@2.5.0
| |   | +-- is-builtin-module@1.0.0
| |   | | `-- builtin-modules@1.1.1
| |   | +-- semver@5.3.0
| |   | `-- validate-npm-package-license@3.0.1
| |   |   +-- spdx-correct@1.0.2
| |   |   | `-- spdx-license-ids@1.2.2
| |   |   `-- spdx-expression-parse@1.0.4
| |   +-- read-pkg-up@1.0.1
| |   | `-- read-pkg@1.1.0
| |   |   +-- load-json-file@1.1.0
| |   |   | +-- parse-json@2.2.0
| |   |   | | `-- error-ex@1.3.1
| |   |   | |   `-- is-arrayish@0.2.1
| |   |   | +-- pify@2.3.0
| |   |   | `-- strip-bom@2.0.0
| |   |   |   `-- is-utf8@0.2.1
| |   |   `-- path-type@1.1.0
| |   +-- redent@1.0.0
| |   | +-- indent-string@2.1.0
| |   | | `-- repeating@2.0.1
| |   | |   `-- is-finite@1.0.2
| |   | |     `-- number-is-nan@1.0.1
| |   | `-- strip-indent@1.0.1
| |   `-- trim-newlines@1.0.0
```

3. Once the project creation and verification is complete, the status of the application is ready, as follows:

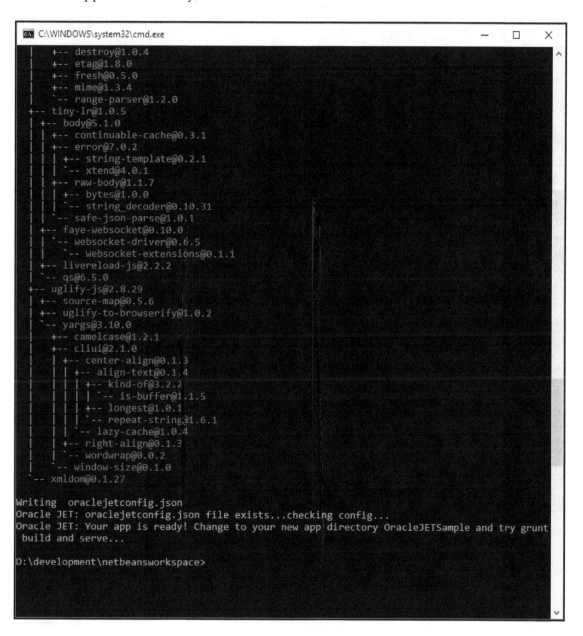

Running a project with Grunt

1. Once the project has been created in the preceding step, it can be built using the following command:

```
cd <project name>
grunt build
```

2. The preceding command should complete the project build, as shown in the following screenshot:

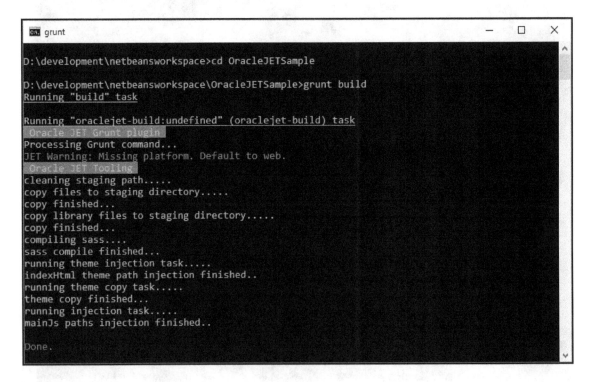

3. Once the project is built successfully, it can be executed using the following command:

```
grunt serve
```

4. The preceding command should run the project, as shown in the following screenshot:

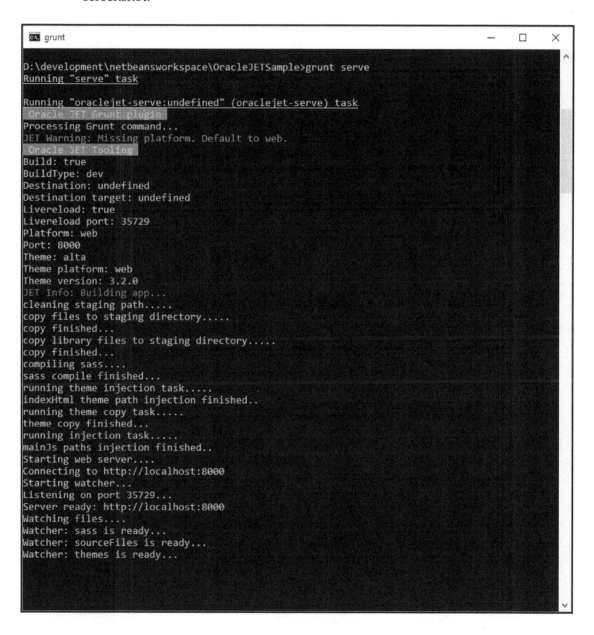

```
grunt                                                          —    □    ×

D:\development\netbeansworkspace\OracleJETSample>grunt serve
Running "serve" task

Running "oraclejet-serve:undefined" (oraclejet-serve) task
Oracle JET Grunt plugin
Processing Grunt command...
JET Warning: Missing platform. Default to web.
Oracle JET Tooling
Build: true
BuildType: dev
Destination: undefined
Destination target: undefined
Livereload: true
Livereload port: 35729
Platform: web
Port: 8000
Theme: alta
Theme platform: web
Theme version: 3.2.0
JET Info: Building app...
cleaning staging path.....
copy files to staging directory.....
copy finished...
copy library files to staging directory.....
copy finished...
compiling sass....
sass compile finished...
running theme injection task.....
indexHtml theme path injection finished..
running theme copy task.....
theme copy finished...
running injection task.....
mainJs paths injection finished..
Starting web server....
Connecting to http://localhost:8000
Starting watcher...
Listening on port 35729...
Server ready: http://localhost:8000
Watching files....
Watcher: sass is ready...
Watcher: sourceFiles is ready...
Watcher: themes is ready...
```

5. Once the project has started running, it should open the application, running in the default browser, as follows:

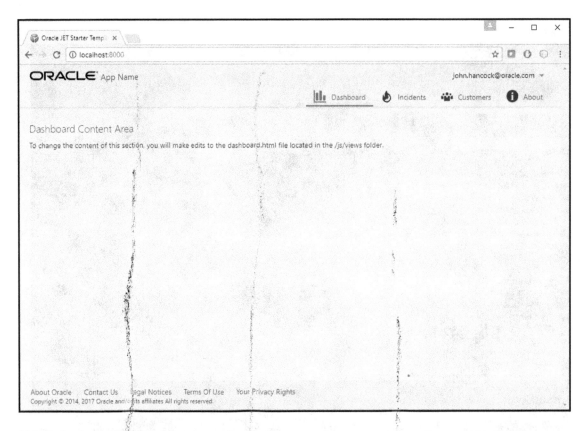

The default application was created using the `navdrawer` template, hence it is showing up with the default `navdrawer` template. We can open the project code in our favorite IDE and edit it to run again using the Grunt `serve` command.

However, the NetBeans IDE is providing the built-in plugins and support for npm and Grunt to manage these build and serve activities within the IDE. In addition, NetBeans provide great syntax advice and support for these plugins. Let's review the IDE installation, configuration, and usage in the following section.

Managing and running the project using NetBeans IDE

NetBeans **Integrated Development Environment** (**IDE**) provides a quick and easy way to develop desktop, mobile, and web applications with Java, JavaScript, HTML5, and other programming languages.

It can be downloaded and installed from its home page: `https://netbeans.org/`.

Once the NetBeans IDE is installed, we can open the project using **File** | **Open Project** and select the project root folder, which opens the project in the IDE as follows:

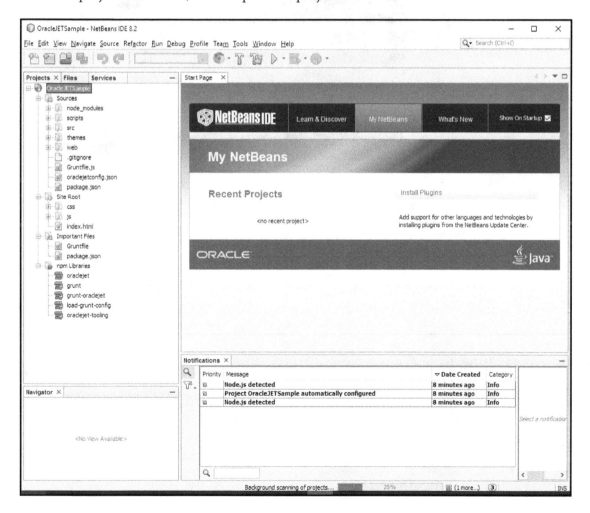

NetBeans automatically identifies this project as an npm Grunt project and shows the directories accordingly. We can expand and review the folder structure.

Right-clicking on the project root folder and selecting the **Build** command (as follows) gives us the option:

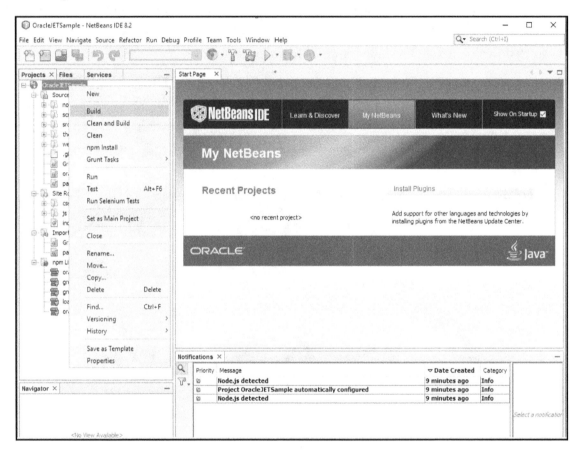

The preceding **Build** option prompts you to configure project actions to call Grunt tasks from within NetBeans IDE. Choose **Yes** to open the configuration window:

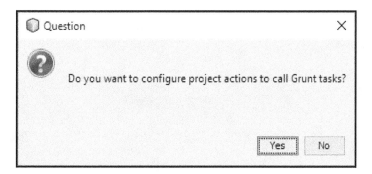

Select all the options (checkboxes) and click **OK** to run Grunt commands enabled in the project actions, as follows:

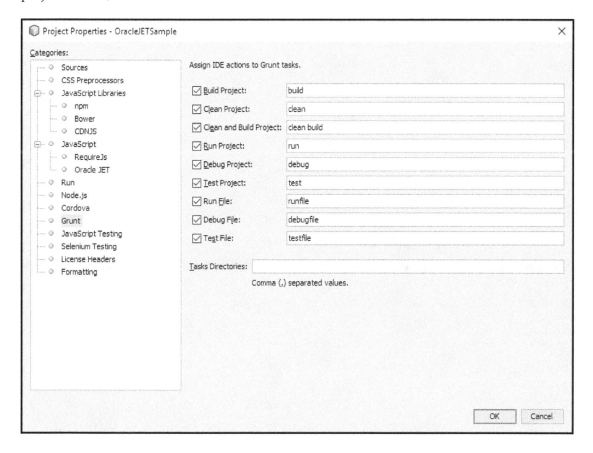

Right-click on the project root folder again and click on the **Build** option to let Grunt build the project within the IDE, as shown in the following screenshot:

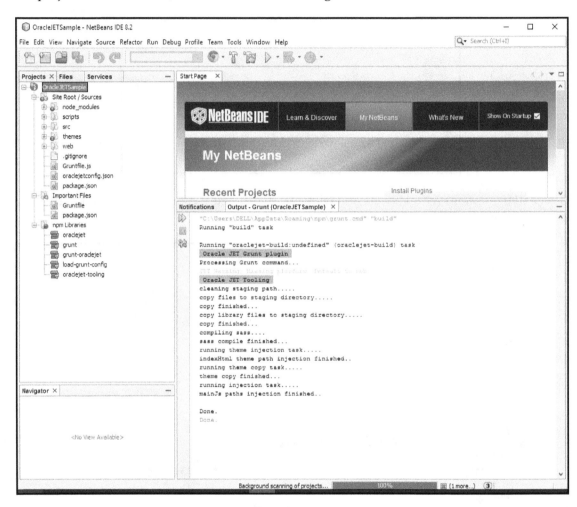

Once the project is built, select the project by clicking on the project root folder, and choose the **Chrome** option from the menu icons as shown in the following screenshot:

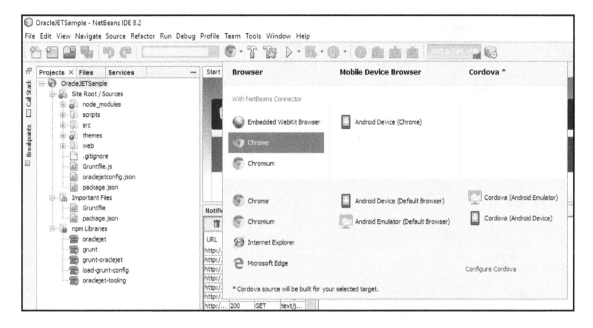

It will prompt you to select the start file; you can choose the `web/index.html` as the start file for the project. Click **OK** to run the project:

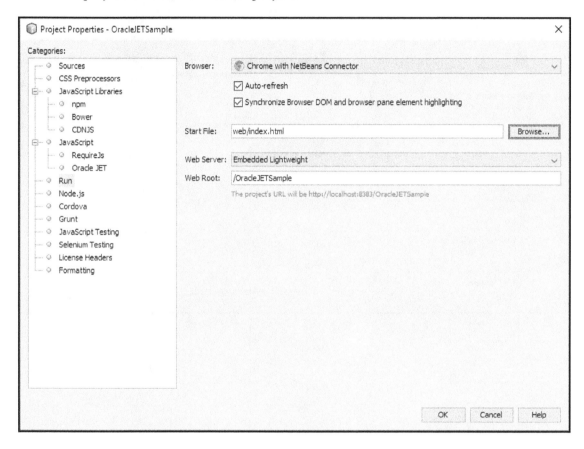

The application should open and run in the Chrome browser (assuming we already have the Chrome browser installed). The first time, it prompts you to install the Chrome NetBeans connector plugin; choose **Yes** to install it. This allows the pages to refresh automatically for future changes, through a NetBeans connection to the browser.

The application should be running and will show the landing page in the browser as follows:

This means that we have successfully built our first Oracle JET application and have run it using both command line and IDE instructions. We can make further changes to the application and observe the changes on web pages, which we will cover in the upcoming chapters.

Summary

Throughout this chapter, we learnt about the essential Oracle JET framework architecture and how it helps us build modern web applications. We also learnt the steps to be followed to generate a template-based, Single-Page Application with the help of tools and techniques including Node.js, npm, Yeoman, Grunt, and Oracle JET generator. We finished this chapter by understanding the NetBeans IDE, managing the project, and building and executing stages from within the IDE.

In the next chapter, we will learn in detail about the Oracle Alta UI framework, used for building the Oracle JET framework.

2
Oracle Alta UI

The process of web development used to include JavaScript and CSS development, but that stopped years ago given the number of web frameworks, templates, and themes available on the market today. The availability of a number of such options allows developers to choose templates and frameworks that match the business context, which also helps them to concentrate more on the data than the presentation layer design and layouts. While each of the JavaScript frameworks has versatile flavors of **User Interface** (**UI**) frameworks, Oracle has developed a standard UI framework that matches both web application and mobile-based application development needs along with cloud application standards, which is called Oracle Alta UI.

In this chapter, we will cover:

- What is Oracle Alta UI?
- Oracle JET web application styles with Alta UI
- Additional page styles and wizards
- Recommendations

What is Oracle Alta UI?

Oracle Alta UI is a set of guidelines and a web design system introduced to help developers build easy, contemporary, and user-friendly GUI applications on both web and mobile platforms. These new web standards introduced by Oracle Alta UI have helped in standardizing the application interface for numerous enterprise applications, including Oracle products and Oracle Cloud native applications. They also helped frameworks such as Oracle ADF and JET with a fresh style, trendy layout, and a consistent look and feel. A lot of effort has been put into building Oracle Alta UI, combining JavaScript, CSS, and UI templates.

Oracle Alta UI does more than just improve the look and feel of an application. It is built based on the following philosophies:

- **Mobile-first approach**: With the aim of supporting both web and mobile platforms, components have been designed to provide users with a large, clear interface with touchscreen capability.
- **Simple and organized layout**: The organized layout helps developers and users to concentrate on the data presented rather than ways to organize the information on a web page.
- **Clear information hierarchy**: The clear information hierarchy enables application usability by giving users an intuitive interface and helping them to figure out what they want and how to navigate through the application effortlessly.
- **Engaging visual content**: A clear and graphical information layout helps users to engage with visual details that clearly distinguish the mobile application from the web application with the responsive web design.

The following diagram represents the features of Oracle Alta UI:

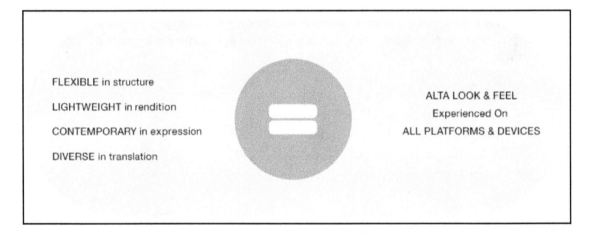

Oracle JET web application styles with Alta UI

Alta UI offers great support through its layout structure and adaptable components for applications to be developed in the Oracle JET framework.

Alta UI divides the page into different layouts that help to fill each section with the respective content to create an organized page structure. The Oracle Alta UI page layout schema can be represented as follows:

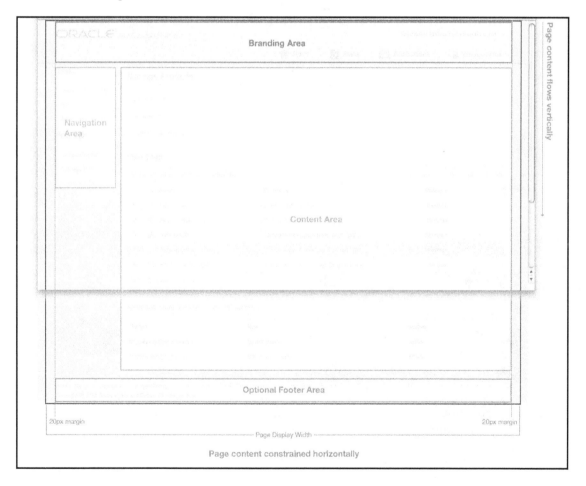

This layout lets us choose the layout that matches our requirements, selecting between branding, menu, content in columns, and footer areas, as represented in the diagram. The following are some of the page layout configurations based on the columns, drawer, and optional footer:

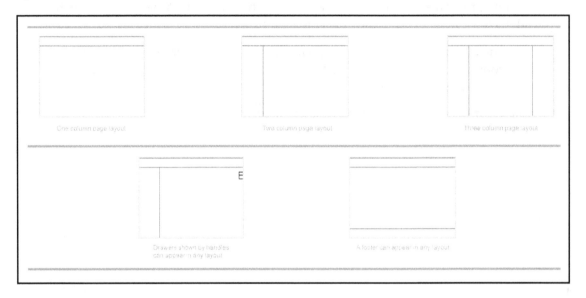

Applications with Alta UI

In this section, let's review a sample web application developed in Oracle JET with Oracle Alta UI. Let's look at the one available for live demo at: `http://www.oracle.com/` `webfolder/technetwork/jet/public_samples/WorkBetter/public_html/index.html`.

Please note that it is assumed that you have already set up the development environment along with the browser plugin as advised in `Chapter 1`, *Getting Started with Oracle JET*. Please complete the setup before running the preceding steps.

We can also download its source code from the website and run it in our development environment, as detailed here:

1. Download the source code from the website `http://www.oracle.com/webfolder/` `technetwork/jet-320/globalExamples-App-WorkBetter.html`. The download page may prompt you for Oracle credentials, which you can obtain by registering with your email.

2. Once the source code (`WorkBetter.zip`) is downloaded, unzip it in your workspace. In case the download is not available from the site, please take it from code samples of this book.

3. From the NetBeans IDE, select the **File** | **Open Project** option and browse to the workspace where you unzipped the *WorkBetter* application.

4. Select the *WorkBetter* application and click on **Open Project** to import the project into NetBeans IDE.

5. Expand the project to review the folder structure containing sources (CSS, JS, SCSS, along with other source code), important files (`package.json`), and npm libraries, as shown in the following screenshot:

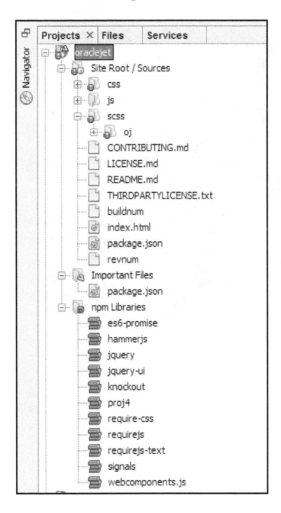

6. Right-click on the project root folder and choose the **Run** option to run the application.

7. The *WorkBetter* application should start running and open the home page on the browser, as shown in the following screenshot:

A thorough review of the code components of this sample application in NetBeans is advised, along with reviewing its features. Let's now review the graphical user interface features on the application home page in the browser. It has the top-level menu options as **Dashboard**, **People**, and **Organization**, with **Dashboard** and **People** as the active tabs.

Dashboard style

A landing page with a dashboard display is the standard dashboard style presented by the Oracle Alta UI framework. It has sections such as **My Organization** with organization statistics, **My Notifications** for the logged-in user, and other crucial information presented as colored tiles that are organized on the page, as shown in the following screenshot. The screenshot from the previous section is repeated here to help you correlate the landing page to the dashboard style:

Card page style

From the dashboard page, by clicking on the top menu option, **People**, the application navigates to the **People** section, which is organized in the **Card** page style layout. On this page, we can see a list of people with icon images and roles, along with their tenure information. The page initially shows 12 people's records; by clicking on the **Show More...** option at the bottom of the page, you can load more records. You can also filter the records with the search box provided. The following is the **Card** page style layout example with Oracle JET:

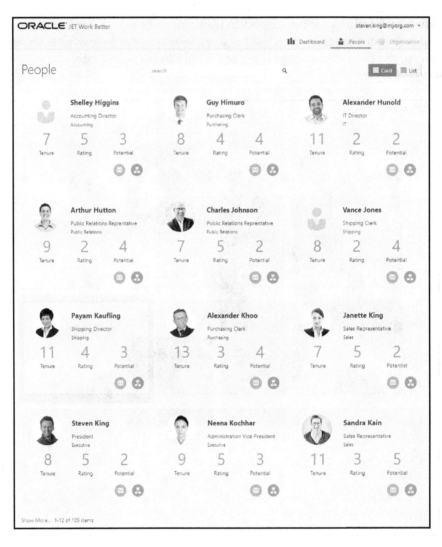

List page style

Within the **People** page, by selecting the **List** option in the top-right corner (next to **Card**), the page layout gets switched to the **List** page style from the **Card** page style.

In the **List** page style, the same set of people's records are displayed as a continuous list with a scroll option and the list keeps growing as you scroll further. The search option still exists to filter the records, as shown in the following screenshot:

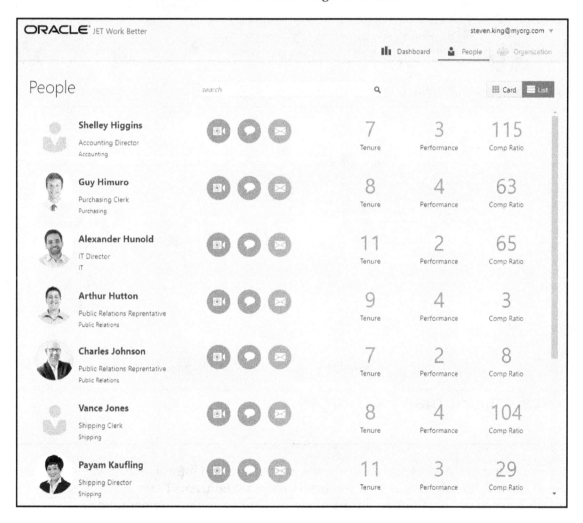

Detail page style

Clicking on any **People** record, either on the **Card** page style or the **List** page style, navigates the application to that specific person's details in the **Detail** page style, as shown in the following screenshot:

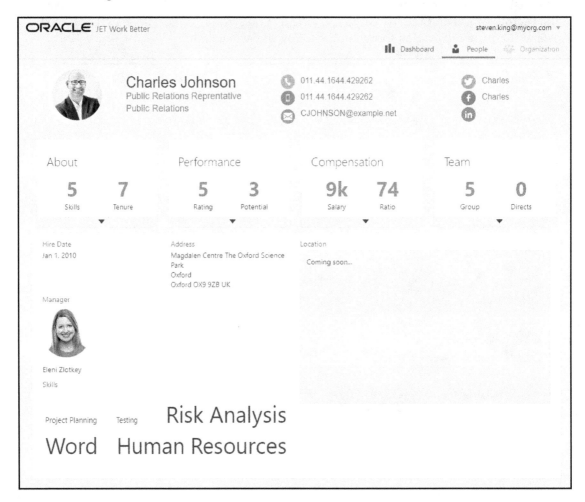

It contains individual contacts, performance, and hierarchical information, along with other person-specific details. **About**, **Performance**, **Compensation**, and **Team** are the tabbed details for each person. Clicking on any of the tabs (for example, **Compensation**) shows the tab-specific information, as follows:

With the preceding sample project, we explored the power of Alta UI and how it makes Oracle JET applications look rich and trendy. While we dig through individual concepts such as components and frameworks in upcoming chapters, we strongly recommend you start reviewing the *WorkBetter* application code in NetBeans IDE, starting from `index.html`, to understand how pages are designed and how the navigation works.

Additional page styles and wizards

Apart from the page styles demonstrated in the preceding sample application, there are a few other important page styles provided by Alta UI. Some of them are detailed as follows:

Form page style

The **Form** page style can contain the information in editable form fields in an organized manner, as shown in the following screenshot:

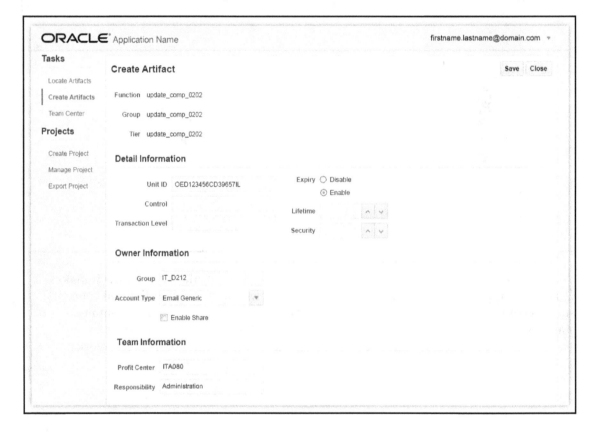

Forms can appear in diverse contexts, including content area, drawer, wizard, or a secondary window.

Master - detail style

To present one-to-many relationship data on the application interface, the **master – detail** style helps with a nice layout (in context), as shown in the following screenshot. They can also appear as drop-down and pop-up styles:

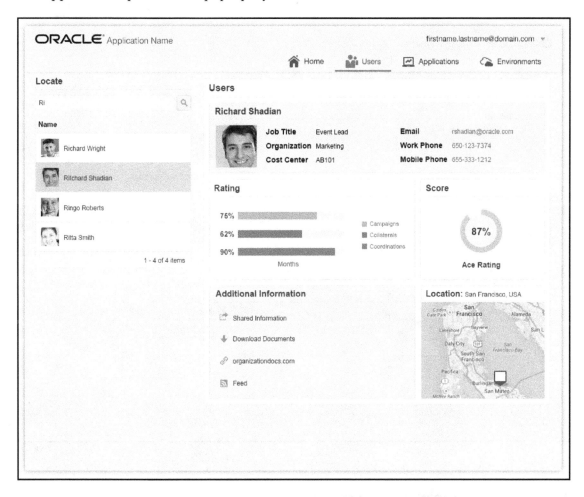

Wizards

When you have a series of tasks to be performed in a step-by-step flow, a wizard is the best choice. Alta UI has a train element to easily navigate and carry out the steps in the wizard view, as shown in the following screenshot:

Recommendations

Along with the previously listed page styles, Alta UI has the capability to customize other sections of the application, such as page attributes, regions, navigation items, data grids, and page layouts, which can be divided into branding, drawer, and footer areas.

While the default theme provided in the following example looks good, you can further customize the application UI design and add many more features with the up-to-date styles, patterns, and options offered by Alta UI, which are available and well documented at the Oracle Alta UI home page: `http://www.oracle.com/webfolder/ux/middleware/alta/index.html`.

In the upcoming chapters, we'll dive deep into detailed concepts, such as components and framework foundations, to be able to effortlessly add fancy features ton our application.

Summary

In this chapter, we learned the essential Oracle Alta UI concepts and about the evolution of Oracle. We also learned about the support Alta UI offers for Oracle JET applications, as well as running through a step-by-step sample web application developed in Oracle JET with Alta UI and reviewing its features in detail. We finished this chapter with an understanding of the power of Alta UI and recommendations for adopting the latest features.

In the next chapter, we will learn about the tool integration that helps to build Oracle JET framework-based applications.

3
Tool Integration

Modern web application development consists of the latest web standards, UI themes, and JavaScript frameworks, while the previous development approaches include keeping the web resources as part of the server-side enterprise application as one of the resources to be loaded from the server. For example, modern web applications in microservice architecture are being built as the web GUI as an exclusive service, while the other server-side components, such as data services, are built as separate service components. The rapid application development needs also pushed for the application build and pipeline to happen quickly, helping the applications release to the market faster.

In this chapter, we will cover the following topics:

- What is the build pipeline?
- Grunt
- Gulp
- RequireJS
- webpack

What is the build pipeline?

Making the web component package an easily deployable set of limited components from the developed resources for easy migration and browser support is the primary goal of build pipeline tools such as Grunt, Gulp, RequireJS, and webpack. During development, we could add a number of additional resources and write the Sass/LeSS content as such.

However, during the application serving phase, wherein the application is run on browser we would want to deliver the content in browser-understandable format. This needs a bit of compilation, a packaging task is involved. The build pipeline addresses such processes seamlessly for diverse frontend technologies used to develop our application.

Please note that either of these tools can help you build and serve your application. You can choose one based on your project needs and prior knowledge.

Syntactically Awesome StyleSheets (Sass) is a scripting language that is interpreted or compiled into **Cascading Style Sheets (CSS)**. SassScript is the scripting language itself.

LESS (Leaner CSS, sometimes stylized as LESS) is a dynamic style sheet language that can be compiled into CSS and run on the client side or server side.

Grunt

As discussed in previous chapters, Grunt helps in automating tedious non-functional activities such as minimization, compilation, unit testing, and linting much more easily. The Grunt ecosystem is growing rapidly, with plugins for your routine tasks including Sass, LESS, RequireJS, and CoffeeScript.

We can install `grunt-cli` using the following command:

```
npm -g install yo grunt-cli
```

If we are using NetBeans IDE for web application development in an Oracle JET project, the build command is essential in making the application complete, although key source files are available in the `src` folder. Grunt tasks, including build and serve, can be enabled within NetBeans IDE to resolve this problem by performing the following steps:

1. Right-click on the project's root folder and select **Build** (as follows), which gives us the option:

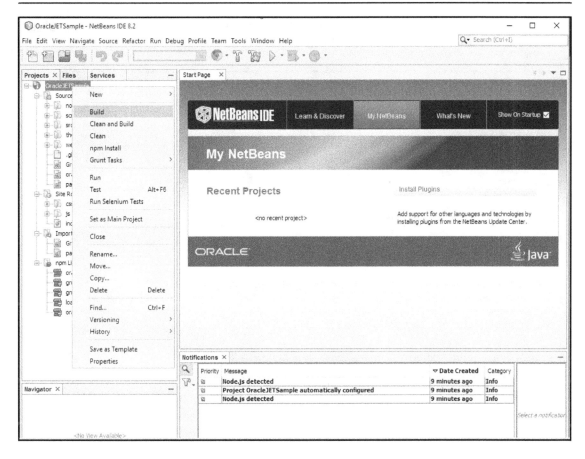

2. The preceding **Build** option prompts you to configure project actions to call Grunt tasks from within NetBeans IDE. Choose **Yes** to open the configuration window:

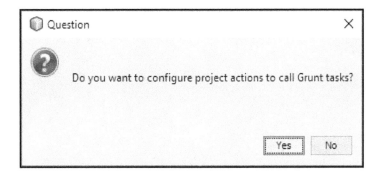

3. Select all the options (checkboxes) and click **OK** to run Grunt commands enabled through project actions as follows:

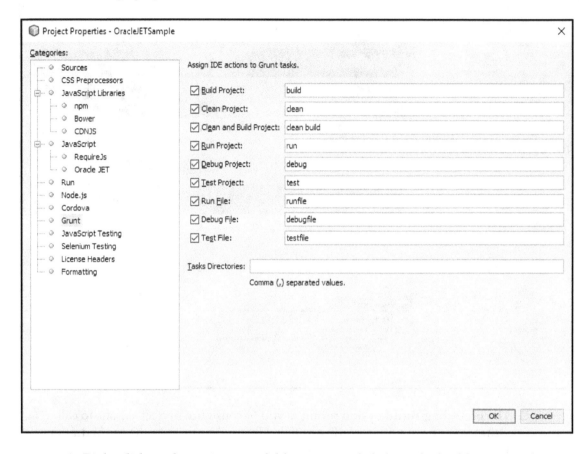

4. Right-click on the project root folder again and click on the build option to let Grunt build the project within the IDE, as shown in the following screenshot:

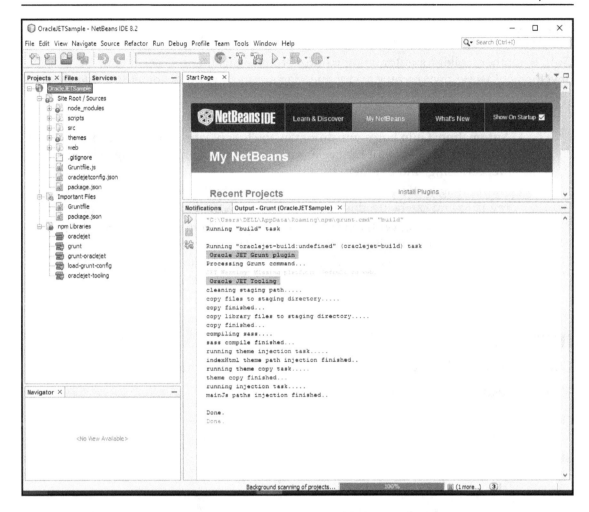

At this point, you need to be very careful. The process above has created a `web` folder. Essentially, developers need to make code changes in the `src` directory, build the application and then run the application from the `web` folder. Do remember this cycle and make sure you always make code changes in the `src` directory only, and if you make changes to the resources under the `web` directory, they will be lost in the next build.

Once `grunt build` is successful and the `web` directory is updated with the latest changes, we can run the `grunt serve` command to deploy the application and review the output on the browser.

Gulp

Gulp is another toolkit for automating painful or time-consuming tasks in your development workflow, so you can stop messing around and build something effortlessly.

The following are the characteristics of the Gulp toolkit:

- **Automation**: Gulp helps you automate the tough, laborious, and repetitive tasks from your development life cycle, such as optimization, minifying, testing, CSS preprocessing, and deploying
- **Platform-agnostic**: Gulp integration support is built and made available with all key IDEs and can be used with Java, Node.js, .NET, PHP and other platforms
- **Strong ecosystem**: With the tremendous support from npm and open source, there are numerous plugins for streaming file transformations
- **Simple**: Gulp is easy to learn and simple to use by offering a nominal API platform

Installing Gulp

Gulp can be installed based on npm using the following command:

```
npm install --global gulp-cli
```

Once the Gulp installation is complete, a `gulpfile.js` configuration file should be generated in the project's `Important Files` folder in NetBeans IDE with its syntax looking like the following:

```
var gulp = require('gulp');
gulp.task('default', function() {
  // place code for your default task here
});
```

Gulp can be executed as part of the command line using the `gulp` command, or made part of the NetBeans IDE commands as follows:

1. The Gulp executable can be configured in NetBeans IDE by selecting **Tools | Options** and choosing the **HTML/JS** and **Gulp** options:

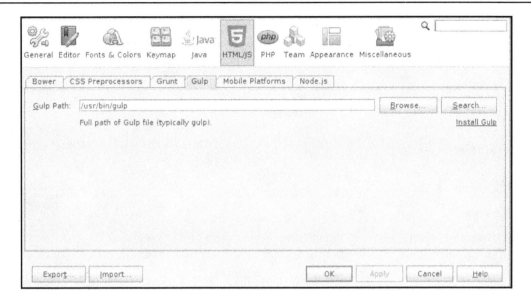

2. The following is the project structure once `gulpfile.js` is added:

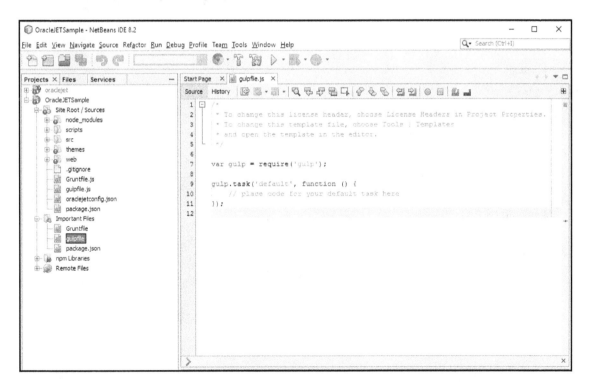

3. Gulp tasks (clean, build, run, debug, and test both project and file, as highlighted in the following screenshot) can be assigned to common IDE actions by right-clicking on the project and selecting the **Project Properties** and **Gulp** options:

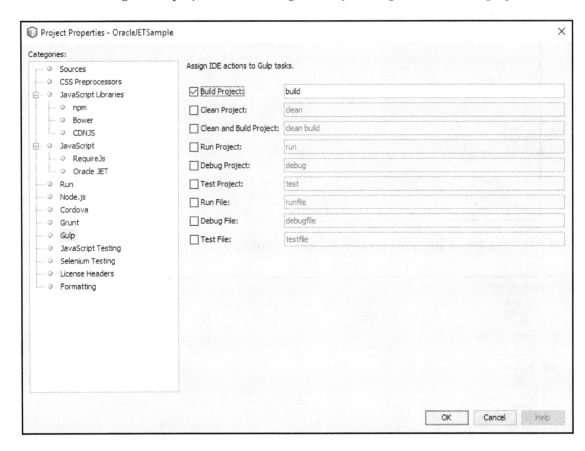

4. Gulp tasks can be run via the project's context menu by right-clicking on the project as follows:

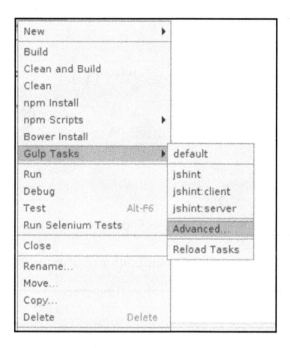

5. We can also set the parameters, if needed, as follows:

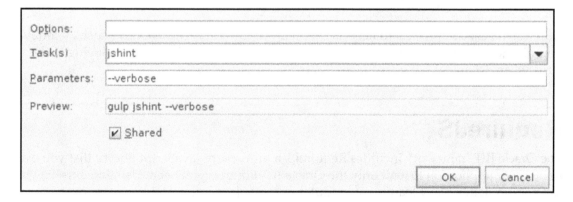

6. We can right-click on the project, select **Gulp Tasks**, and click the saved advanced option to invoke the target to execute as follows:

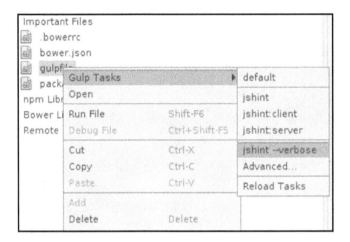

7. Gulp output can be reviewed in the output window as the script is executed:

```
Starting 'jshint:client'...
Starting 'jshint:server'...
Finished 'jshint:client' after 92 ms
Finished 'jshint:server' after 127 ms
Starting 'jshint'...
Finished 'jshint' after 7.2 µs
```

Gulp can be used in projects to help us save a lot of effort in repetitive tasks such as code optimization, minifying, programmatic testing, CSS preprocessing, and deploying to the targeted environment.

RequireJS

The Oracle JET framework includes RequireJS, a third-party JavaScript library that you can use in your application to load only the Oracle JET libraries you need. Using RequireJS, you can also implement lazy loading of modules or create JavaScript partitions that contain more than one module.

The asynchronous module loading and dependency management can be handled by RequireJS as it implements the **Asynchronous Module Definition** (AMD) API.

> AMD is a specification for the programming language JavaScript. It defines an application programming interface (API) that defines code modules and their dependencies, and loads them asynchronously if desired.

Installing RequireJS

To set up RequireJS for managing application libraries, links, and script references in your Oracle JET application, you can perform the following steps:

1. Download RequireJS from its home page: `http://requirejs.org/docs/download.html`.

2. Include RequireJS in your application home page as follows:

```
<html>
  <head>
    <script data-main="js/main" src="js/require.js"></script>
  </head>
  <body> <h1>Require JS with Oracle JET </h1> </body>
</html>
```

Here, the `data-main` attribute refers to the `main.js` dependency represented as `js/main`.

3. From here on, we can include the dependencies for each module explicitly as follows:

```
// +js/main.js
require(["js/customers"], function(cust) {
  cust.createCustomers();
});

// +js/customers.js
define(["js/orders"], function(ord) {
  return function createCustomer() {
    ord.raiseOrder();
  }
}

// +js/orders.js
define(function() {
```

```
   return function raiseOrder() {
     // doSomething
   }
 }
```

4. We can add any application startup code to the callback function. For example, a knockout binding call to the callback function for the `dialogWrapper` element is added in the following snippet:

```
require(['app', 'ojs/ojcore', 'knockout', 'jquery',
         'ojs/ojmodel', 'ojs/ojknockout-model', 'ojs/ojdialog'],
function(app, oj, ko) // obtaining a reference to the oj namespace
{
   ko.applyBindings(new app()/*View Model instance*/,
                 document.getElementById('dialogWrapper'));
}
);
```

5. We can also include the path of the resource bundles to be merged with our application as follows:

```
config: {
  ojL10n: {
    merge: {
      'ojtranslations/nls/ojtranslations':
      'resources/nls/myTranslations'
    }
  }
}
```

The `oj` namespace is reserved by the Oracle JET framework, meaning we cannot use the same namespace in our Oracle JET application code. The `oj` namespace is defined in the `ojs/ojcore` module, and other modules which are loaded after oj belongs to the objects from them inside the `oj` namespace.

The following table shows the list of Oracle JET modules along with usage advice:

Oracle JET Module	Description	When to Use?
ojs/ojcore	Core framework module that defines a base Oracle JET object. Includes support for prototype-based JavaScript object inheritance and extending JavaScript objects by copying their properties. The module returns oj namespace. You must include this module in any Oracle JET application.	Always
ojs/ojmodel	Oracle JET's Common Model	Use if your application uses the Oracle JET Common Model.
ojs/ojknockout-model	Utilities for integrating Oracle JET's Common Model into Knockout.js	Use if your application uses the Oracle JET Common Model, and you want to integrate with Knockout.js.
ojs/ojvalidation	Data validation and conversion services	Use if your application uses Oracle JET validators or converters outside of Oracle JET editable components.
ojs/ojknockout-validation	Support for the invalidComponentTracker binding option on input components	Use if your application uses validators or converters, and you want to track the validity of the Oracle JET components in your application.
ojs/ojcomponent: Examples: ojs/ojbutton ojs/ojtoolbar ojs/ojtabs	Oracle JET component modules. Most Oracle JET components have their own module with the same name in lowercase, except for the following components: ojButtonset: ojs/ojbutton ojInputPassword: ojs/ojinputtext ojTextArea: ojs/ojinputtext ojCombobox: ojs/ojselectcombobox ojSelect: ojs/ojselectcombobox ojSparkChart: ojs/ojchart ojDialGauge: ojs/ojgauge ojLedGauge: ojs/ojgauge ojRatingGauge: ojs/ojgauge ojStatusMeterGauge: ojs/ojgauge	Use component modules that correspond to any Oracle JET component in your application.
ojs/ojknockout	Oracle JET ojComponent binding and services for Knockout.js	Use if your application includes Oracle JET components and you want to use ojComponent binding for these components in Knockout.js.
ojs/ojrouter	Class for managing routing in single page applications	Use if your single page application uses oj.Router for routing.
ojs/ojmodule	Binding for Knockout.js that implements navigation within a region of a single page application	Use if your single page application uses the ojModule binding for managing content replacement within a page region.
ojs/ojoffcanvas	Methods for controlling off-canvas regions	Use if your application uses oj.offCanvasUtils for managing off-canvas regions.
ojs/ojcube	Class for aggregating data values in ojDataGrid	Use if your application renders aggregated cubic data in an ojDataGrid component.

You can observe that RequireJS is already included in the sample project you set up in multiple places. For example, expand the source folders and you can see the RequireJS entry in `index.html` as follows:

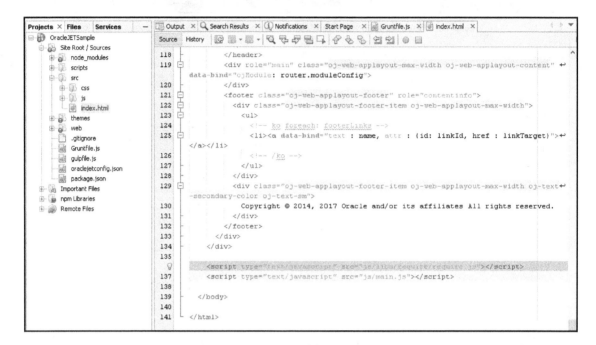

Also, the Grunt file with build and serve tasks includes only the required modules, as shown in the following screenshot:

webpack

The webpack is another of the latest open source JavaScript module bundlers. The webpack takes modules with dependencies and generates static assets representing those modules.

Long-term caching of static assets with webpack is a great way to package all your static resources such as JavaScript, CSS, or even images, but to effectively use generated assets in production, one should leverage long-term caching.

As shown in the following figure, webpack helps bundle all the modules with dependencies including **.sass** and **.hbs** files for **.css**, and makes static assets deliver as deployable applications:

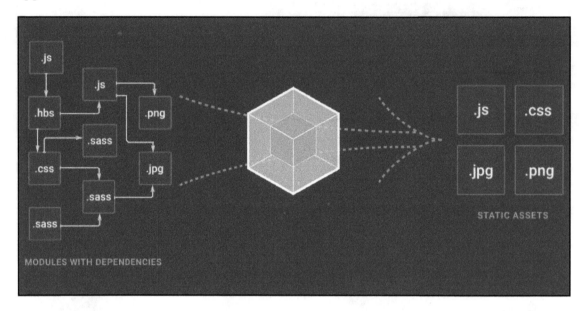

The webpack is available to work in two modes: CLI and API.

Use the **command-line interface** (**CLI**) to configure and interact with your build. This is mostly useful in case of early prototyping, profiling, writing npm scripts, or personal customization of the build.

API includes the Node and Module Loader plugins for webpack:

1. The first step to make webpack part of your build process is to install it through npm. Run either of the following commands:

```
npm install --save-dev webpack
npm install --save-dev webpack@<version>
```

2. To make webpack available globally, you can give the install command as follows:

```
npm install --global webpack
```

3. Import the dependencies of one script file into another based on relationship using an import statement. Let's say you have `hello.js` as the JavaScript file with all the dependencies.

4. Expect to bundle the webpack into the `dist/bundle.js` file and make the `bundle.js` entry into your HTML file.

5. You can run webpack with this script file reference to generate the bundle as follows:

```
./node_modules/.bin/webpack src/hello.js dist/bundle.js
```

6. Now if you run your HTML page, it should serve with the bundle file dependency added successfully.

7. Instead of step 5, you can also bundle webpack using config file/npm style. Please refer to the webpack documentation at `https://webpack.js.org/guides/getting-started/` for more details.

Summary

In this chapter, we learned the essential Oracle JET build concepts and the support from industry leading build tools. We also learned about the support for Oracle JET application building with modern build tools such as Grunt, Gulp, and RequireJS. We finished this chapter with an understanding of the webpack API and how it helps bundle the modules with dependencies into static assets to serve web applications efficiently.

In the next chapter, we will learn about the role of Knockout.js in Oracle JET application architecture and application development in detail.

4
Knockout JS

The evolution of web application development has been helping application development to become easier, faster, and more efficient. While the newer frameworks are helping to build efficient applications on top of them, they are also helping developers by taking care of the data binding part from the model to the view layer on client-side architecture. These data binding techniques are adopted in Oracle JET as well, with the help of the entire Knockout.js framework. Frameworks such as Knockout are helping developers to concentrate on the data and business on the pages while they are taking care of component binding and managing the respective dependencies.

In this chapter, we will cover the following topics:

- What is Knockout.js?
- Installation and programming
- Observables
- Data bindings
- External data access and animations
- Usage in Oracle JET applications

What is Knockout.js?

Knockout.js is a JavaScript library that provides a cleaner way to manage the changes across the View, ViewModel, and Model to seamlessly reflect the changes between the layers with the help of two-way data bindings. This way, the developers don't have to worry about the handling of data updates between the JavaScript objects and the HTML view objects; instead, a data binding is established between the JavaScript objects and the view renderers, so that the updates are communicated by the framework, leaving us to concentrate on the data model and business logic behind the application.

The purpose of the Knockout.js library is to help design scalable, data-driven interfaces, but it does not attempt to be an alternative to standard frameworks such as jQuery or prototype.

In this chapter, let's review the features and components of Knockout.js that help Oracle JET handle the JavaScript MVVM architecture efficiently.

The **View, View Model** and **Model** responsibilities are represented in the following diagram:

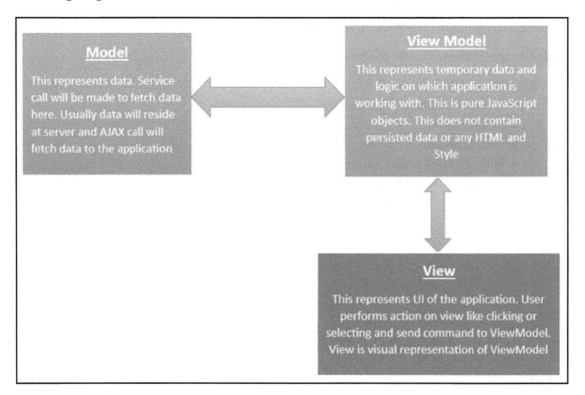

Knockout.js features

Knockout.js offers diverse features for application development, including the following:

- **Language**: As the Knockout.js framework is written with pure JavaScript, it is easily rendered on most browsers, and gels up easily with server-side technologies such as Java, .NET, RoR, or PHP
- **Declarative bindings**: Knockout.js allows developers to easily associate the model with the DOM elements using a readable and concise syntax
- **Automatic view refresh**: With the two-way binding, the changes on the data model automatically update the view components (HTML UI) with the newer values
- **Dependency management**: Dependencies between the model data are implicitly managed to combine and transform as needed
- **UI template**: Rapid template generation for the data model-driven UI component tree structure
- **Extensibility**: Along with the number of reusable components delivered, Knockout.js lets developers produce custom components based on application needs with bindings
- **Utilities**: To help map the server data to the HTML page rendering in a generic way, the framework offers a set of utility functions, including JSON parsers and array handlers

> For this chapter, we will create a new project called `KnockoutJSExample` to learn about Knockout.js, and get back to our `OracleJETExample` project to learn how Knockout.js is used in Oracle JET.

Installation and programming

The following are the series of steps involved in Knockout.js installation and usage:

1. Create a new web application in NetBeans using the options **File** | **New Project**. This opens the **New Project** wizard, as shown in the following screenshot:

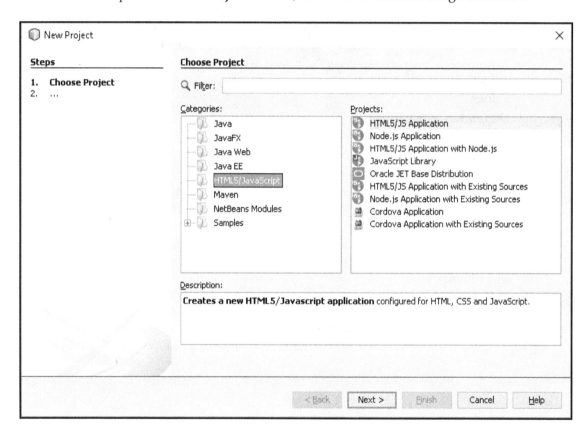

2. Press **Next** to provide the name and location of the project, as shown in the following screenshot:

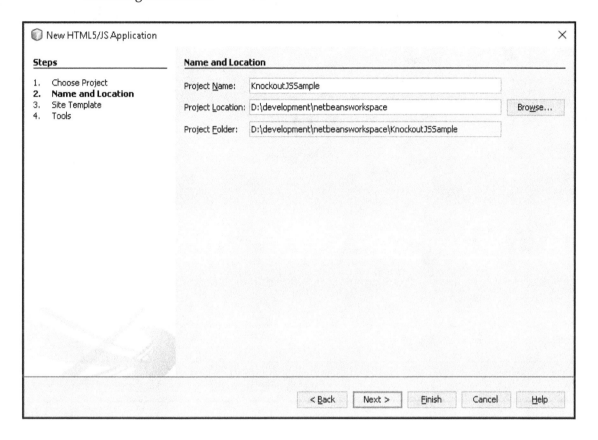

3. Enter the **Project Name** and select the **Next** option to select the site template; choose **No Site Template**, as shown in the following screenshot:

4. Click the **Next** button to select the build package tools including `package.json`, `bower.json`, `Gruntfile.js`, and `gulpfile.js`, as shown in the following screenshot:

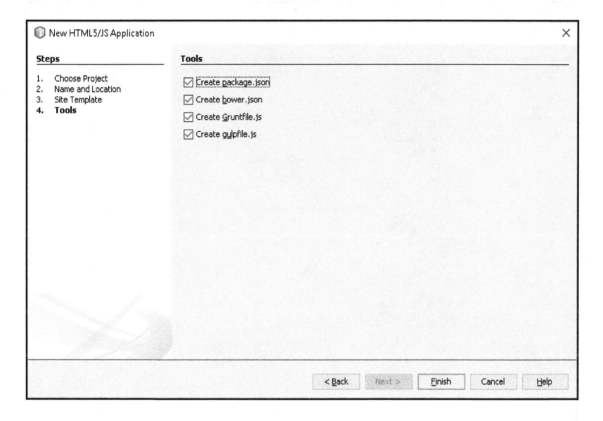

5. Click on **Finish** to create the project and show the `index.html` page, as shown in the following screenshot:

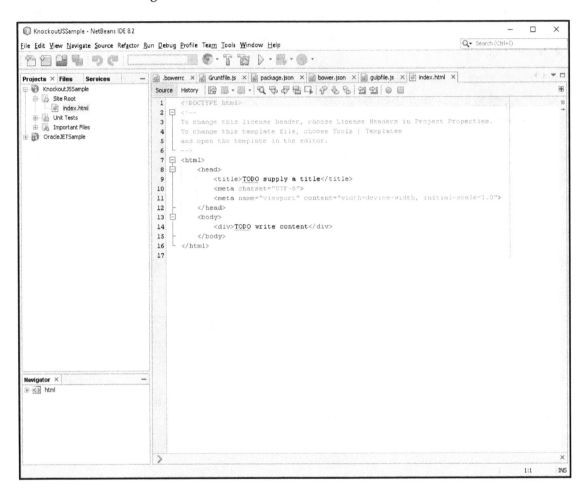

6. Right-click on the `Site Root` folder and choose **New Folder** to create a directory for JavaScript files, as shown in the following screenshot:

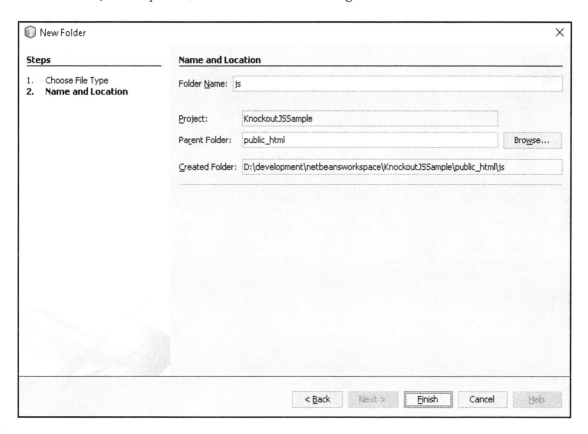

7. Download the latest version of Knockout.js (3.4.2 at the time of writing), which is available for download at the official website: `http://knockoutjs.com/downloads/index.html`. Save it (`knockout-3.4.2.js`) into the `js` folder you created in the preceding step.

8. Refresh the project to see the Knockout.js library added to the project, as shown in the following screenshot:

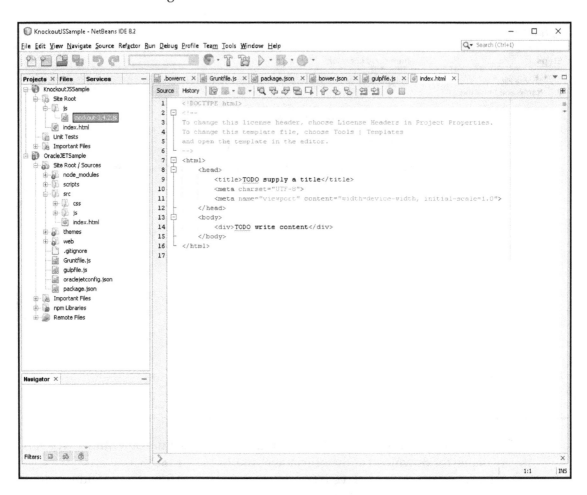

9. With the preceding structure in place, write the following content as
   `index.html`. You can observe the `employeeViewModel` object content from the
   JavaScript that is added to the Knockout bindings, which is accessible by the UI
   components through the `data-bind` attribute on the HTML elements:

```html
<!DOCTYPE html>
<html>
  <head>
    <title>Knockout JS</title>
  </head>
  <body>
    <h1>Welcome to Knockout JS programming</h1>
    <table border="1" >
      <tr >
        <th colspan="2" style="padding:10px;">
          <b>Employee Data from View Model</b>
        </th>
      </tr>
      <tr>
        <td style="padding:10px;">Employee First Name:</td>
        <td style="padding:10px;">
          <span data-bind='text: empFirstName'></span>
        </td>
      </tr>
      <tr>
        <td style="padding:10px;">Employee Last Name:</td>
        <td style="padding:10px;">
          <span data-bind='text: empLastName'></span>
        </td>
      </tr>
    </table>
    <!-- JavaScript resources -->
    <script type='text/javascript' src='js/knockout-3.4.2.js'>
    </script>
    <script type='text/javascript'>
      var employeeViewModel = {
        empFirstName: "Tony",
        empLastName: "Henry"
      };
      ko.applyBindings(employeeViewModel);
      // ko stands for knockout js object
    </script>
  </body>
</html>
```

10. Right-click on the project and click on the **Run** command to serve the application from NetBeans, as follows:

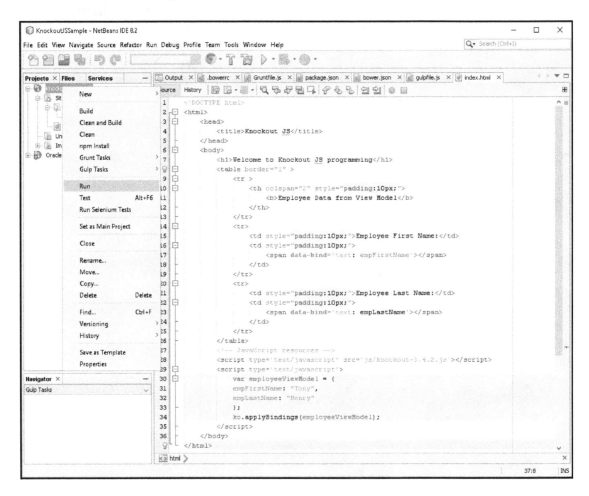

11. The application should run through the port and show the browser with the home page containing the content loaded from the view model, as shown in the following screenshot:

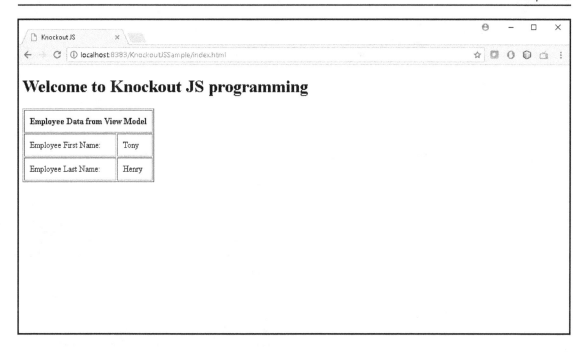

Observables

Any property that you want to track the changes and let the view components automatically update needs to be added as an observable. This will let you dynamically change the value of the properties added to a view model based on several operations and data exchange through interactions.

Let us review an example of adding a property to our previous program with the observable ability, as follows:

1. Change the index.html page content to include an additional property organizationName with observable nature, as follows:

```
<!DOCTYPE html>
<html>
  <head>
    <title>Knockout JS</title>
  </head>
  <body>
    <h1>Welcome to Knockout JS programming</h1>
    <table border="1" >
      <tr >
```

```
                  <th colspan="2" style="padding:10px;">
                    <b>Employee Data - Organization :
                      <span style="color:red"
                             data-bind='text: organizationName'>
                      </span>
                    </b>
                  </th>
                </tr>
                <tr>
                  <td style="padding:10px;">Employee First Name:</td>
                  <td style="padding:10px;">
                    <span data-bind='text: empFirstName'></span>
                  </td>
                </tr>
                <tr>
                  <td style="padding:10px;">Employee Last Name:</td>
                  <td style="padding:10px;">
                    <span data-bind='text: empLastName'></span>
                  </td>
                </tr>
              </table>
              <!-- JavaScript resources -->
              <script type='text/javascript' src='js/knockout-3.4.2.js'>
              </script>
              <script type='text/javascript'>
                var employeeViewModel = {
                  empFirstName: "Tony",
                  empLastName: "Henry",
                  organizationName: ko.observable("Sun")
                };
                ko.applyBindings(employeeViewModel);
                employeeViewModel.organizationName("Oracle");
              </script>
            </body>
          </html>
```

2. From the preceding program, you can observe that the `organizationName` value is added as `Sun` when it is initially added to the Knockout bindings. Through the program, the value is later changed to `Oracle`. However, when the page content is loaded, we can observe that the value of the `organizationName` is rendered as `Oracle` on the table header, as follows:

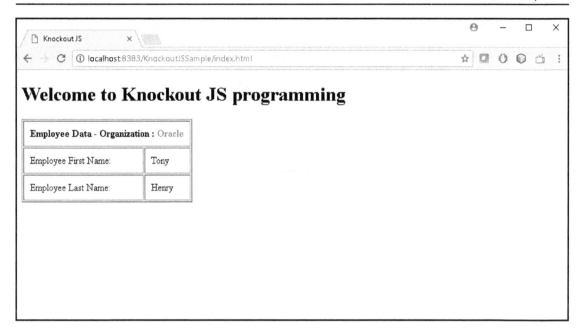

Computed observables

A computed observable is a property that is created by dynamically generating the value depending on the other properties. This means several other observables contribute to generate the value of this computed observable. Hence, a change in any of the dependent observables is expected to cause the computed observable value to be updated and reflected in the view bindings.

From the preceding example, add another variable called orgFullName, which adds a suffix to the organizationName as Limited. The interesting part is, as and when you update the organizationName value based on the program (for example, to Oracle in our case), you can observe that the orgFullName value gets updated as well (to Oracle Limited in our case).

The following is the full program for index.html:

```
<!DOCTYPE html>
<html>
  <head>
    <title>Knockout JS</title>
  </head>
  <body>
    <h1>Welcome to Knockout JS programming</h1>
```

```
    <table border="1" >
      <tr>
        <th colspan="2" style="padding:10px;">
          <b>Employee Data - Organization :
            <span style="color:red" data-bind='text: organizationName'>
            </span>
          </b>
        </th>
      </tr>
      <tr>
        <td style="padding:10px;">Employee First Name:</td>
        <td style="padding:10px;">
          <span data-bind='text: empFirstName'></span>
        </td>
      </tr>
        <tr>
          <td style="padding:10px;">Employee Last Name:</td>
          <td style="padding:10px;">
            <span data-bind='text: empLastName'></span>
          </td>
        </tr>
      </table>
      <p>Organization Full Name :
        <span style="color:red" data-bind='text: orgFullName'></span>
      </p>

      <!-- JavaScript resources -->
      <script type='text/javascript' src='js/knockout-3.4.2.js'></script>
      <script type='text/javascript'>
        var employeeViewModel = {
          empFirstName: "Tony",
          empLastName: "Henry",
          organizationName: ko.observable("Sun")
        };
        employeeViewModel.orgFullName = ko.computed(function() {
          return employeeViewModel.organizationName() + " Limited";
        });
        ko.applyBindings(employeeViewModel);
        employeeViewModel.organizationName("Oracle");
      </script>
    </body>
</html>
```

The following is the page rendered with observable and computed observable variables:

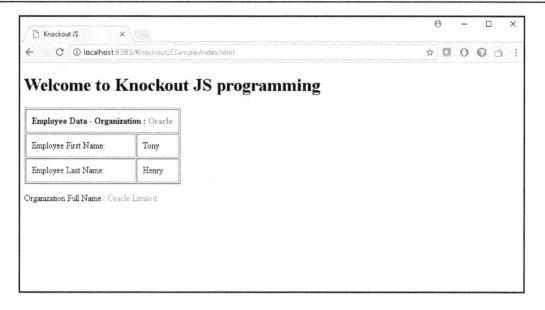

Observable arrays

Observable arrays let us define a list of items as an observable item so that the object-changing values get reflected in the view components. Let us review this scenario with an example:

1. We will add a function `Employee` and an `observableArray` organization to the page, and try to load the `Employee` array in the page as a table. For this, include the following web page content to the `index.html` page:

```
<!DOCTYPE html>
<html>
  <head>
    <title>Knockout JS</title>
  </head>
  <body>
    <h1>Welcome to Knockout JS programming</h1>
    <table border="1" >
      <tr >
        <th colspan="2" style="padding:10px;">
          <b>Employee Data - Organization :
            <span style="color:red"
                  data-bind='text: organizationName'>
            </span>
          </b>
```

```
        </th>
      </tr>
      <tr>
        <td style="padding:10px;">Employee First Name:</td>
        <td style="padding:10px;">
          <span data-bind='text: empFirstName'></span>
        </td>
      </tr>
      <tr>
        <td style="padding:10px;">Employee Last Name:</td>
        <td style="padding:10px;">
          <span data-bind='text: empLastName'></span>
        </td>
      </tr>
    </table>
    <p>Organization Full Name :
      <span style="color:red" data-bind='text: orgFullName'>
      </span>
    </p>
    <!-- Observable Arrays-->
    <h2>Observable Array Example : </h2>
    <table border="1">
      <thead><tr>
        <th style="padding:10px;">First Name</th>
        <th style="padding:10px;">Last Name</th>
      </tr></thead>
      <tbody data-bind='foreach: organization'>
        <tr>
          <td style="padding:10px;" data-bind='text: firstName'>
          </td>
          <td style="padding:10px;" data-bind='text: lastName'>
          </td>
        </tr>
      </tbody>
    </table>

    <!-- JavaScript resources -->
    <script type='text/javascript' src='js/knockout-3.4.2.js'>
    </script>
    <script type='text/javascript'>
      function Employee (firstName, lastName) {
        this.firstName = ko.observable(firstName);
        this.lastName = ko.observable(lastName);
      };
      var employeeViewModel = {
        empFirstName: "Tony",
        empLastName: "Henry",
        //Observable
```

```
        organizationName: ko.observable("Sun"),
        //Observable Arrays

        organization : ko.observableArray([
          new Employee("John", "Kennedy"),
          new Employee("Peter", "Hennes"),
          new Employee("Richmond", "Smith")
        ])
      };
      //Computed Observable
      employeeViewModel.orgFullName = ko.computed(function() {
        return employeeViewModel.organizationName() + " Limited";
      });
      ko.applyBindings(employeeViewModel);
      employeeViewModel.organizationName("Oracle");

    </script>
  </body>
</html>
```

2. Run the preceding page to see the observable array on the browser, as follows:

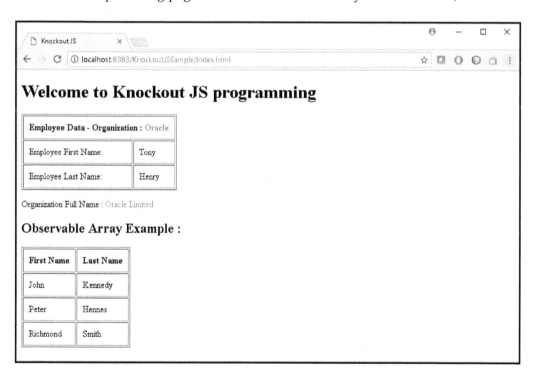

3. We can also write a function that can add rows to this observable array dynamically. For this, let's add two text fields, `newFirstName` and `newLastName`, which are defined as observable in the `EmployeeViewModel`. We have added a new function (`addEmployee`) which gets invoked on a button click, and adds a new row to the organization observable array as a new `Employee` by taking the values from the `newFirstName` and `newLastName` form fields. Copy the following program to `index.html` to run this example:

```html
<!DOCTYPE html>
<html>
  <head>
    <title>Knockout JS</title>
  </head>
  <body>
    <h1>Welcome to Knockout JS programming</h1>
    <table border="1" >
      <tr >
        <th colspan="2" style="padding:10px;">
          <b>Employee Data - Organization :
            <span style="color:red"
                  data-bind='text: organizationName'>
            </span>
          </b>
        </th>
      </tr>
      <tr>
        <td style="padding:10px;">Employee First Name:</td>
        <td style="padding:10px;">
          <span data-bind='text: empFirstName'></span>
        </td>
      </tr>
      <tr>
        <td style="padding:10px;">Employee Last Name:</td>
        <td style="padding:10px;">
          <span data-bind='text: empLastName'></span>
        </td>
      </tr>
    </table>
    <p>Organization Full Name :
      <span style="color:red" data-bind='text: orgFullName'>
      </span>
    </p>
    <!-- Observable Arrays-->
    <h2>Observable Array Example : </h2>
      <table border="1">
      <thead><tr>
```

```
      <th style="padding:10px;">First Name</th>
      <th style="padding:10px;">Last Name</th>
  </tr></thead>
  <tbody data-bind='foreach: organization'>
    <tr>
      <td style="padding:10px;" data-bind='text: firstName'>
      </td>
      <td style="padding:10px;" data-bind='text: lastName'>
      </td>
    </tr>
  </tbody>
</table>
<h2>Add New Employee to Observable Array</h2>
  First Name : <input data-bind="value: newFirstName" />
  Last Name : <input data-bind="value: newLastName" />
  <button data-bind='click: addEmployee'>Add Employee</button>
  <!-- JavaScript resources -->
  <script type='text/javascript' src='js/knockout-3.4.2.js'>
  </script>
  <script type='text/javascript'>
    function Employee (firstName, lastName) {
      this.firstName = ko.observable(firstName);
      this.lastName = ko.observable(lastName);
    };
    this.addEmployee = function() {
      this.organization.push(new Employee
          (employeeViewModel.newFirstName(),
           employeeViewModel.newLastName()));
    };
    var employeeViewModel = {
      empFirstName: "Tony",
      empLastName: "Henry",
      //Observable
      organizationName: ko.observable("Sun"),
      newFirstName: ko.observable(""),
      newLastName: ko.observable(""),
      //Observable Arrays
      organization : ko.observableArray([
        new Employee("John", "Kennedy"),
        new Employee("Peter", "Hennes"),
        new Employee("Richmond", "Smith")
      ])
    };
    //Computed Observable
    employeeViewModel.orgFullName = ko.computed(function() {
      return employeeViewModel.organizationName() + " Limited";
    });
    ko.applyBindings(employeeViewModel);
```

```
            employeeViewModel.organizationName("Oracle");
        </script>
      </body>
    </html>
```

4. Run the application to see the page loaded with new form fields, as follows:

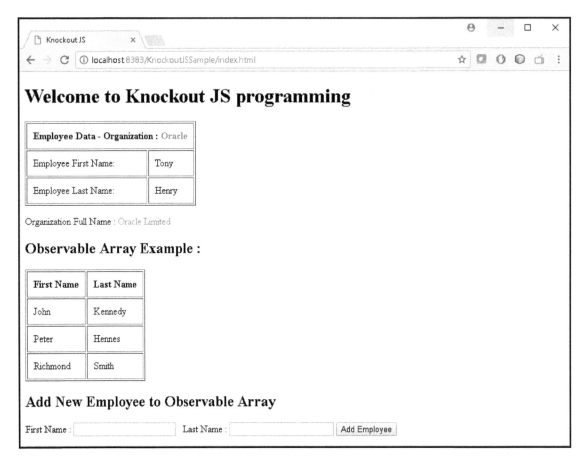

5. Add a new employee first name and last name in the text fields that appear at the bottom, then click on the **Add Employee** button to add a new row to the Observable array table, as follows:

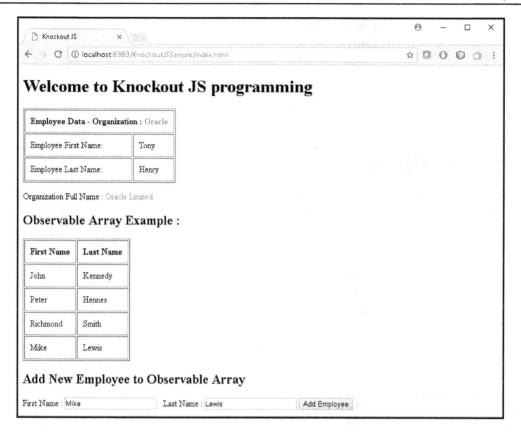

You will have observed that in the example, we have used the push() method to add a new row to the array object. The following is a list of the observable array methods supported by Knockout.js:

- push(): Adds a new item to the end of the array
- pop(): Removes the last value from the array and returns it
- unshift(): Inserts a new item at the beginning of the array
- shift(): Removes the first value from the array and returns it
- splice(): Removes and returns a given number of elements starting from a given index
- remove(): Removes all values that equal some items, and returns them as an array
- removeAll(): Removes all values and returns them as an array
- destroy(): Finds any objects in the array that equal some items, and gives them a special property called _destroy with value true

- destroyAll(): Gives a special property called _destroy with value true to all objects in the array
- sort(): Sorts the array contents and returns the observableArray
- indexOf(): The indexOf function returns the index of the first array item that equals your parameter

Data bindings

Data bindings are attributes added by the framework for the purpose of data access between elements and view scope. While Observable arrays are efficient in accessing the list of objects with the number of operations on top of the display of the list using the foreach function, Knockout.js has provided three additional data binding abilities:

- Control-flow bindings
- Appearance bindings
- Interactive bindings

Let us review these data bindings in detail in the following sections.

Control-flow bindings

As the name suggests, control-flow bindings help us access the data elements based on a certain condition. The if, if-not, and with are the control-flow bindings available from the Knockout.js.

In the following example, we will be using if and with control-flow bindings. We have added a new attribute to the Employee object called age; we are displaying the age value in green only if it is greater than 20. Similarly, we have added another markedEmployee. By this, with control-flow binding, we can limit the scope of access to that specific employee object in the following paragraph. Add the following code snippet to index.html and run the program to see the if and with control-flow bindings working:

```
<!DOCTYPE html>
<html>
  <head>
    <title>Knockout JS</title>
  </head>
  <body>
    <h1>Welcome to Knockout JS programming</h1>
    <table border="1" >
```

```
    <tr >
      <th colspan="2" style="padding:10px;">
        <b>Employee Data - Organization :
          <span style="color:red" data-bind='text: organizationName'>
          </span>
        </b>
      </th>
  </tr>
  <tr>
    <td style="padding:10px;">Employee First Name:</td>
    <td style="padding:10px;">
      <span data-bind='text: empFirstName'></span>
    </td>
    </tr>
      <tr>
        <td style="padding:10px;">Employee Last Name:</td>
        <td style="padding:10px;">
          <span data-bind='text: empLastName'></span>
        </td>
    </tr>
</table>
<p>Organization Full Name :
    <span style="color:red" data-bind='text: orgFullName'></span>
</p>
<!-- Observable Arrays-->
<h2>Observable Array Example : </h2>
<table border="1">
    <thead><tr>
      <th style="padding:10px;">First Name</th>
      <th style="padding:10px;">Last Name</th>
      <th style="padding:10px;">Age</th>
    </tr></thead>
    <tbody data-bind='foreach: organization'>
      <tr>
        <td style="padding:10px;" data-bind='text: firstName'></td>
        <td style="padding:10px;" data-bind='text: lastName'></td>
        <td data-bind="if: age() > 20"
            style="color: green;padding:10px;">
          <span data-bind='text:age'></span>
        </td>
      </tr>
    </tbody>
</table>
<!-- with control flow bindings -->
<p data-bind='with: markedEmployee'>
    Employee <strong data-bind="text: firstName() + ', ' + lastName()">
    </strong> is marked with the age <strong data-bind='text: age'>
    </strong>.
```

```
    </p>
    <h2>Add New Employee to Observable Array</h2>
    First Name : <input data-bind="value: newFirstName" />
    Last Name : <input data-bind="value: newLastName" />
    Age : <input data-bind="value: newEmpAge" />
    <button data-bind='click: addEmployee'>Add Employee</button>
    <!-- JavaScript resources -->
    <script type='text/javascript' src='js/knockout-3.4.2.js'></script>
    <script type='text/javascript'>
      function Employee (firstName, lastName,age) {
        this.firstName = ko.observable(firstName);
        this.lastName = ko.observable(lastName);
        this.age = ko.observable(age);
      };
      this.addEmployee = function() {
        this.organization.push(new Employee
            (employeeViewModel.newFirstName(),
             employeeViewModel.newLastName(),
             employeeViewModel.newEmpAge()));
      };
      var employeeViewModel = {
        empFirstName: "Tony",
        empLastName: "Henry",
        //Observable
        organizationName: ko.observable("Sun"),
        newFirstName: ko.observable(""),
        newLastName: ko.observable(""),
        newEmpAge: ko.observable(""),
        //With control flow object
        markedEmployee: ko.observable(new Employee("Garry", "Parks",
                                                   "65")),
        //Observable Arrays
        organization : ko.observableArray([
          new Employee("John", "Kennedy", "24"),
          new Employee("Peter", "Hennes","18"),
          new Employee("Richmond", "Smith","54")
        ])
      };
      //Computed Observable
      employeeViewModel.orgFullName = ko.computed(function() {
        return employeeViewModel.organizationName() + " Limited";
      });
      ko.applyBindings(employeeViewModel);
      employeeViewModel.organizationName("Oracle");
    </script>
  </body>
</html>
```

Run the preceding program to see the `if` control-flow acting on the `Age` field, and the `with` control-flow showing a marked employee record with age `65`:

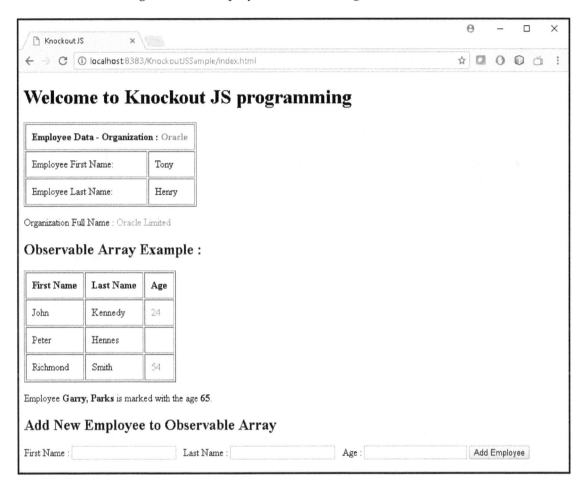

Appearance bindings

Appearance bindings deal with displaying the data from binding elements on view components in formats such as text and HTML, and applying styles with the help of a set of six bindings, as follows:

- Text: `<value>`—Sets the value to an element. Example:

```
<td data-bind='text: name'></td>
```

- HTML: `<value>`—Sets the HTML value to an element. Example:

```
//JavaScript:
function Employee(firstname, lastname, age) {
  ...
  this.formattedName = ko.computed(function() {
    return "<strong>" + this.firstname() + "</strong>";
  }, this);
}

//Html:
<span data-bind='html: markedEmployee().formattedName'></span>
```

- Visible: `<condition>`—An element can be shown or hidden based on the condition. Example:

```
<td data-bind='visible: age() > 20' style='color: green'>
    span data-bind='text:age'>
```

- CSS: `<object>`—An element can be associated with a CSS class. Example:

```
//CSS:
.strongEmployee {
  font-weight: bold;
}


//HTML:
<span data-bind='text: formattedName, css: {strongEmployee}'>
</span>
```

- Style: `<object>`—Associates an inline style to the element. Example:

```
<span data-bind='text: age,
      style: {color: age() > 20 ? "green" :"red"}'>
</span>
```

- Attr: `<object>`—Defines an attribute for the element. Example:

```
<p><a data-bind='attr: {href: featuredEmployee().populatelink}'>
    View Employee</a></p>
```

Interactive bindings

Interactive bindings help the user interact with the form elements to be associated with corresponding viewmodel methods or events to be triggered in the pages. Knockout JS supports the following interactive bindings:

- Click: `<method>`—An element click invokes a ViewModel method. Example:

  ```
  <button data-bind='click: addEmployee'>Submit</button>
  ```

- Value: `<property>`—Associates the form element value to the ViewModel attribute. Example:

  ```
  <td>Age: <input data-bind='value: age' /></td>
  ```

- Event: `<object>`—With an user-initiated event, it invokes a method. Example:

  ```
  <p data-bind='event: {mouseover: showEmployee,
                        mouseout: hideEmployee}'>
  Age: <input data-bind='value: Age' /> </p>
  ```

- Submit: `<method>`—With a form submit event, it can invoke a method. Example:

  ```
  <form data-bind="submit: addEmployee">
    <!—Employee form fields -->
    <button type="submit">Submit</button>
  </form>
  ```

- Enable: `<property>`—Conditionally enables the form elements. Example: last name field is enabled only after adding first name field.
- Disable: `<property>`—Conditionally disables the form elements. Example: last name field is disabled after adding first name:

  ```
  <p>Last Name:
    <input data-bind='value: lastName, disable: firstName' />
  </p>
  ```

- Checked: `<property>`—Associates a checkbox or radio element to the ViewModel attribute. Example:

  ```
  <p>Gender: <input data-bind='checked:gender' type='checkbox' /></p>
  ```

- Options: `<array>`—Defines a ViewModel array for the `<select>` element. Example:

```
//Javascript:
  this.designations = ko.observableArray(['manager',
                                          'administrator']);

//Html:
  Designation: <select data-bind='options: designations'></select>
```

- selectedOptions: `<array>`—Defines the active/selected element from the `<select>` element. Example:

```
Designation: <select data-bind='options: designations,
              optionsText:"Select",
              selectedOptions:defaultDesignation'>
</select>
```

- hasfocus: `<property>`—Associates the focus attribute to the element. Example:

```
First Name: <input data-bind='value: firstName,
              hasfocus: firstNameHasFocus' />
```

External data access and animations

Knockout JS can easily integrate with any of the open source frameworks seamlessly to achieve the business requirement. For external data access, we can use jQuery methods such as `$.getJSON()` and `$.post()` to populate the content from external source, or invoke jQuery animation methods for onscreen animations.

For example, if your HTML element has to load employee information from an external `source`on button click, call a Knockout function first, within which you can invoke jQuery methods, as follows:

1. The following code is the HTML part:

```
<p><button data-bind='click: loadEmployee'>Load Data
</button></p>
```

2. JavaScript:

```
self. loadEmployee = function() {
  $.getJSON("/get-employee", function(data) {
    employeeViewModel.firstName=data.firstName;
```

```
      });
  }
```

Usage in Oracle JET applications

Knockout JS has been extensively used in Oracle JET for data binding and page rendering responsibilities. We can review the sample project created for Oracle JET for the Knockout JS usage. While there are a number of places in the sample project that refer to Knockout, the following is one quick reference where you can see the usage of observables for data bindings.

Open the `OracleJETSample` project we created in previous chapters, and access the `appController.js` component under `src/js/appController.js`.

You can see that Knockout is used for the data bindings with `observable` and `observableArray` to populate the application username, login details, and application reference links as follows:

Similarly, references to Knockout JS can be found in HTML page bindings such as `data-bind`, and events such as a button click on `index.html`, as follows:

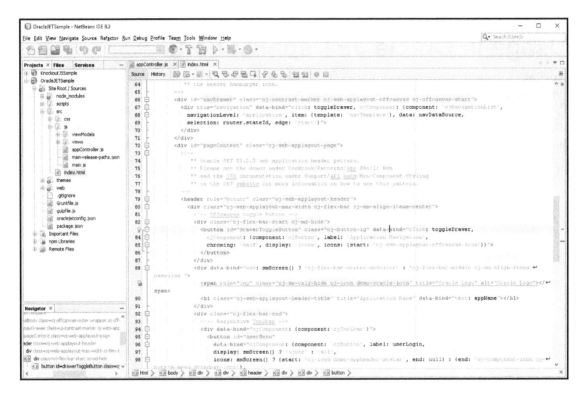

Summary

In this chapter, we learned about the features of the JavaScript data binding library Knockout JS, which is extensively used in Oracle JET. We also learned about the installation and sample project creation with Knockout JS and reviewed features such as observables, data bindings, and external data access with examples. We finished this chapter with an understanding of how Knockout JS is extensively used in Oracle JET for data bindings with observable array component references from a sample application.

In the next chapter, we will learn about Oracle JET components such as collections, controls, and forms in detail.

5
Oracle JET Components – Form Elements, Controls, and Data Collections

The web application development with Oracle JET framework involves the use of various Oracle JET components provided by the framework, including the forms, controls, and data collection components. In the previous chapter, we learned how Knockout framework helps us with data bindings and data access to Oracle JET components. The way to include these components in our application is usually simple and straightforward, it includes adding the element and attaching the state to the element to make it an active part of the application life cycle.

In this chapter, we will cover:

- Oracle JET components
- Steps involved in adding a component
- Form elements
- Form controls
- Data collections

Oracle JET components

As a framework, Oracle JET offers several components with patterns and utility functions. To associate the state to these components, they wrap over the jQuery UI widgets including methods and events. This lets the components benefit from the two-way binding feature from Knockout.js, as discussed in the previous chapter. However, the Oracle JET components adopt only limited and required sets of jQuery UI modules.

Oracle JET components are developed by extending the simple HTML components. Out of the following listed Oracle JET components, some of the simple components, such as `ojInputText` and `ojTable`, extend a single HTML component such as input and table, while a few other components are developed by extending more than one HTML component, such as `ojButton`, which extends multiple HTML components: `input`, `div`, and `button`.

Oracle JET components share a common functionality by providing support for methods such as `getNodebySubId()`, `getSubIdByNode()`, `getContextByNode()`, and options such as root attributes, keyboard navigation support, and component state change.

Following are some of the key components of the Oracle JET framework, along with the corresponding API provided by the framework:

Sr. No	Component Name	Corresponding API
1	**Accordion**	`ojAccordion`
2	Button	`ojButton`
3	Button set	`ojButtonset`
4	Chart	`ojChart`
5	Checkbox set	`ojCheckboxset`
6	Collapsible	`ojCollapsible`
7	Combobox	`ojCombobox`
8	Conveyor belt	`ojConveyorBelt`
9	Data grid	`ojDataGrid`
10	Date and time picker	`ojInputDateTime`
11	Date picker	`ojInputDate`
12	Diagram	`ojDiagram`
13	Dial gauge	`ojDialGauge`
14	Dialog	`ojDialog`
15	Drawer utilities	`oj.OffcanvasUtils`
16	Film strip	`ojFilmstrip`
17	Input number	`ojInputNumber`

Sr. No	Component Name	Corresponding API
18	Input password	ojInputPassword
19	LED gauge	ojLEDGauge
20	Legend	ojLegend
21	List view	ojListView
22	Masonry layout	ojMasonryLayout
23	Menu	ojMenu
24	Nav list	ojNavigationList
25	Nbox	ojNBox
26	Pagination	ojPagingControl
27	Popup	ojPopup
28	Progress indicator	ojProgressbar
29	Radioset	ojRadioset
30	Rating gauge	ojRatingGauge
31	Row expander (Tree table)	ojRowExpander
32	Select	ojSelect
33	Slider	ojSlider
34	Spark chart	ojSparkChart
35	Status meter gauge	ojStatusMeterGauge
36	Sunburst	ojSunburst
37	Switch	ojSwitch
38	Table	ojTable
39	Tabs	ojTabs
40	Tag cloud	ojTagCloud
41	Text area	ojTextArea
42	Textbox	ojInputText
43	Thematic map	ojThematicMap
44	Time picker	ojInputTime
45	Timeline	ojTimeLine
46	Toolbar	ojToolbar
47	Train	ojTrain
48	Tree	ojTree
49	Tree map	ojTreemap

Steps involved in adding a component

Now that we understand the list of components offered by the Oracle JET framework, let's review the steps involved in adding these components to the application before looking at the syntax and usage of these components in groups as follows:

1. Create a web application for Oracle JET, as discussed in the `Chapter 1`, *Getting Started with Oracle JET*.

2. Based on your requirements, choose the set of Oracle JET components you need for your application.

3. Include the components to your page, along with Knockout data binding to associate the state for components. For example, refer to the `dateTime` component as follows:

```
<div id="div5">
  <label for="dateTime">Date and Time</label>
  <input id="dateTime5"
    data-bind= "ojComponent: {component: 'ojInputDateTime',
    value: value}"/>
    <br/>
    <span class="oj-label">Date Time Selected:</span>
    <span data-bind="text: value"></span>
</div>
```

4. Associate the components added from step 3 to the state by selectively including the RequireJS mappings. For example, follow the script function with RequireJS for the `datetime` element added in step 3:

```
require(['ojs/ojcore', 'knockout', 'jquery', 'ojs/ojknockout',
         'ojs/ojdatetimepicker'],
function (oj, ko, $)
{
  function SimpleModel()
  {
    this.value = ko.observable(oj.IntlConverterUtils
                    .dateToLocalIso(new Date(2017, 10, 10)));
  }
  $(document).ready(function ()
  {
    ko.applyBindings(new SimpleModel(),
                    document.getElementById('div5'));
  });
});
```

Form components

Form components are the rich UI components delivered by the Oracle JET framework to help interact with the user in an intuitive and enterprise-standard application theme. Let's review the Oracle JET form elements in groups based on the nature of the elements.

Text input components

Text input components are the components which extend the standard HTML input and text area elements. Oracle JET text input components include input text, password, text area, number, date, time, and date time.

Input text

Create an `ojInputText` component using the `ojComponent` binding with an ID. To review the value of the text element, create an HTML label with the `for` attribute referring to the value of ID from `ojInputText`. Populate the value from the model layer. The following is the example for the text input component:

- **HTML:**

```html
<div id="divId">
  <label for="text-input">First Name</label>
  <input id="text-input" type="text" data-bind="ojComponent:
   {component: 'ojInputText', value: firstName}"/>
  <br/>
  <span class="oj-label">First Name value is: </span>
  <span data-bind="text: firstName"></span>
</div>
```

- **JavaScript:**

```javascript
require(['ojs/ojcore', 'knockout', 'jquery', 'ojs/ojknockout',
         'ojs/ojinputtext'],
function (oj, ko, $)
{
  function SimpleModel()
  {
    this.firstName = ko.observable("Richard");
  };
  $(function ()
  {
    ko.applyBindings(new SimpleModel(),
```

```
                                        document.getElementById('divId'));
        });
    });
```

The output should be displayed on the page as follows:

First Name

Richard

First Name value is:

Richard

You can change the value of the text field (`First Name`) and see the label value underneath changing simultaneously as the two-way data binding is enabled through Knockout.js. Additionally, it supports setting the component width, showing as read only or disabled field, converter, and setting a label for this field based on identifier.

Input password

Create an `ojInputPassword` component using the `ojComponent` binding with an ID. To review the value of a password element, create an HTML label with the `for` attribute referring to the value of ID from `ojInputPassword`. Populate the value from the model layer. The following is the example for the password component:

- **HTML:**

```
<div id="divId">
  <label for="pwd">Password:</label>
  <input type="password" id="pwd" data-bind="ojComponent:
  {component: 'ojInputPassword', value: secret}"/>
  <br/><br/>
  <span class="oj-label">Password value entered: </span>
  <span data-bind="text: secret"></span>
</div>
```

- **JavaScript**:

```
require(['ojs/ojcore', 'knockout', 'jquery', 'ojs/ojknockout',
         'ojs/ojinputtext'],
function (oj, ko, $)
{
  function SimpleModel()
  {
    this.secret = ko.observable("secret text");
  };
  $(function ()
  {
    ko.applyBindings(new SimpleModel(),
                     document.getElementById('divId'));
  });
});
```

The output should be displayed in the page as follows:

Password:

•••••••••••

Password value entered:

secret text

You can change the value of the password field and see the label value underneath changing simultaneously as the two-way data binding is enabled through Knockout JS. Additionally, it supports setting the component width, showing as a read only or disabled field, and restricting password patterns.

Text area

Create an `ojTextArea` component using the `ojComponent` binding with an ID. To review the value of the text area element, create an HTML label with the `for` attribute referring to the value of ID from `ojTextArea`. Populate the value from the model layer. The following is the example for the text area component:

- **HTML**:

```
<div id="divId">
  <label for="resizableDesc">Description:</label>
  <textarea id="resizableDesc" style="resize: both;"
```

```
      data-bind="ojComponent: {component: 'ojTextArea',
      value: desc}" ></textarea>
      <br/><br/>
      <span class="oj-label">Description value is:</span>
      <span data-bind="text: desc"></span>
</div>
```

- **JavaScript**:

```
require(['ojs/ojcore', 'knockout', 'jquery', 'ojs/ojknockout',
          'ojs/ojinputtext'],
function (oj, ko, $)
{
  function SimpleModel()
  {
    this.desc = ko.observable("longer description");
  };
  $(function ()
  {
    ko.applyBindings(new SimpleModel(),
                     document.getElementById('divId'));
  });
});
```

The output should be displayed on the page as follows:

You can change the value of the text area (description) field and see the label value underneath changing simultaneously as the two-way data binding is enabled through Knockout.js. Moreover, this text area can be resized by dragging the right bottom corner of the text area. Additionally, it supports setting the component width, showing as a read only or disabled field.

Input number

Create an `ojInputNumber` component using the `ojComponent` binding with an ID. To review the value of the number element, create an HTML label with the `for` attribute referring to the value of the ID from `ojInputNumber`. Populate the value from the model layer. The following is the example for the input number component:

- **HTML**:

```
<form id="form1">
  <label for="age">Age:</label>
  <input id="age" data-bind="ojComponent:
                    {component: 'ojInputNumber', max:max, min:min,
                     step:step, value:currentAge}"/>
  <br/> <hr/>
  <span>Age value is: </span>
  <span id="curr-value" data-bind="text: currentAge"></span>
</form>
```

- **JavaScript**:

```
require(['ojs/ojcore', 'knockout', 'jquery', 'ojs/ojknockout',
        'ojs/ojinputnumber'],
function(oj, ko, $)
{
  function InputNumberModel(){
    self = this;
    self.currentAge = ko.observable(30);
    self.max = ko.observable(100);
    self.min = ko.observable(0);
    self.step = ko.observable(1);
  }
  var inputNumberModel = new InputNumberModel();
  $(function()
  {
    ko.applyBindings(inputNumberModel,
                    document.getElementById('form1'));
  });
});
```

The output should be displayed on the page as follows:

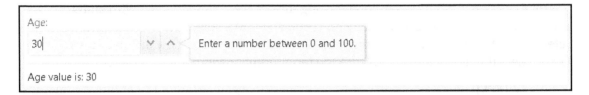

You can change the value of the number (Age) field and see the label value underneath changing simultaneously between the minimum and maximum value assigned, as shown in the preceding screenshot. Additionally, it supports setting the step value, converter, validator, and restrict-only numbers.

Input date

Create an `ojInputDate` component using the `ojComponent` binding with an ID. To review the value of the `date` element, create an HTML label with the `for` attribute referring to the value of the ID from `ojInputDate`. Populate the value from the model layer:

- **HTML:**

```html
<div id="divId">
  <label for="joiningDate">Joining Date:</label>
  <input id="joiningDate" data-bind="ojComponent:
   {component: 'ojInputDate', value: doj}"/>
  <br/><br/>
  <span class="oj-label">Joining Date value is: </span>
  <span data-bind="text: doj"></span>
</div>
```

- **JavaScript:**

```javascript
require(['ojs/ojcore', 'knockout', 'jquery', 'ojs/ojknockout',
        'ojs/ojdatetimepicker', 'ojs/ojselectcombobox',
        'ojs/ojtimezonedata'],
function (oj, ko, $)
{
  function SimpleModel()
  {
    this.doj = ko.observable(oj.IntlConverterUtils.dateToLocalIso
                        (new Date(2017, 10, 10)));
  };
  $(function ()
  {
```

```
        ko.applyBindings(new SimpleModel(),
                        document.getElementById('divId'));
    });
});
```

As you try to select a new value for the date, the output should be displayed on the page as follows:

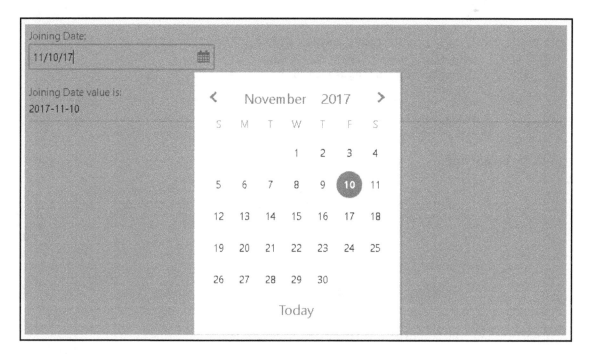

You can change the value of the date (**Joining Date**) field and see the label value underneath changing simultaneously, based on the date picker selection. Additionally, it supports setting the converter, restricting the date range, selecting a date range, letting us select across months and a particular week of the year.

Input time

Create an `ojInputTime` component using the `ojComponent` binding with an ID. To review the value of the time element, create an HTML label with the `for` attribute referring to the value of the ID from `ojInputTime`. Populate the value from the model layer:

- **HTML**:

```
<div id="divId">
  <label for="eventTime">Event Time:</label>
  <input id="eventTime" data-bind="ojComponent:
  {component: 'ojInputTime', value: eventTm }"/>
  <br/><br/>
  <span class="oj-label">Event Time value is:</span>
  <span data-bind="text: eventTm"></span>
</div>
```

- **JavaScript**:

```
require(['ojs/ojcore', 'knockout', 'jquery', 'ojs/ojknockout',
         'ojs/ojdatetimepicker', 'ojs/ojselectcombobox',
         'ojs/ojtimezonedata'],
function (oj, ko, $)
{
  function SimpleModel()
  {
    this.eventTm = ko.observable(oj.IntlConverterUtils
              .dateToLocalIso(new Date(2017, 10, 10, 5, 10)));
  };
  $(function ()
  {
    ko.applyBindings(new SimpleModel(),
                     document.getElementById('divId'));
  });
});
```

As you try to select a new value for the time, the output should be displayed on the page as follows:

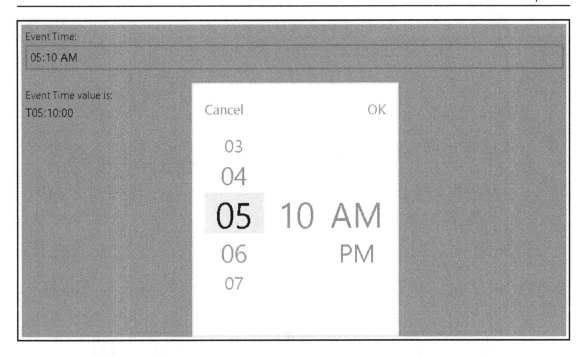

You can change the value of the time (**Event Time**) field and see the label value changing simultaneously, based on the time picker selection. Additionally, it supports setting the custom validators and increments on other page events.

Input date time

Create an `ojInputDateTime` component using the `ojComponent` binding with an ID. To review the value of the date time element, create an HTML label with the `for` attribute referring to the value of the ID from `ojInputDateTime`. Populate the value from the model layer. The following is the example for the date time input component:

- **HTML**:

```
<div id="divId">
   <label for="birthDateTime">Birth Date Time:</label>
   <input id="birthDateTime" data-bind="ojComponent: {component:
        'ojInputDateTime', value: bdt}"/>
   <br/><br/>
   <span class="oj-label">Current component value is:</span>
   <span data-bind="text: bdt"></span>
</div>
```

- **JavaScript**:

```
require(['ojs/ojcore', 'knockout', 'jquery', 'ojs/ojknockout',
         'ojs/ojdatetimepicker', 'ojs/ojtimezonedata'],
function (oj, ko, $)
{
  function SimpleModel()
  {
    this.bdt = ko.observable(oj.IntlConverterUtils
             .dateToLocalIso(new Date(2017, 10, 10, 5, 10)));
  }
  $(function ()
  {
    ko.applyBindings(new SimpleModel(),
                     document.getElementById('divId'));
  });
});
```

As you try to select a new value for the date time, the output should be displayed on the page as follows:

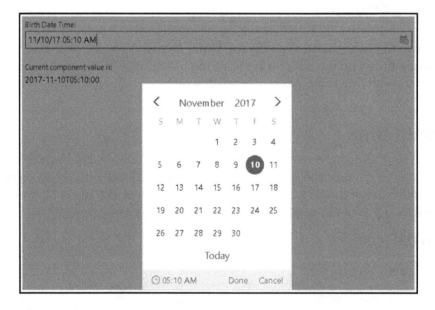

You can change the value of the date time (**Birth Date Time**) field and see the label value underneath changing simultaneously, based on the date time picker selection. Additionally, it supports setting the timezone, validators, and customizing the widget.

Selection components

Selection components are the components that let us select one or more values from the set of available values. Oracle JET selection components include select, combobox, checkbox, radio, and switch.

Select

Create an `ojSelect` component using the `ojComponent` binding with an ID. To review the value of the `select` element, create an HTML label with the `for` attribute referring to the value of the ID from `ojSelect`. Populate the value from the model layer.

The `select` component is available in two modes, single select and multi select. Let's look at examples for both. Following is the example for the single select component:

- **HTML (single select)**:

```
<form id="form1">
  <label for="selectTransport">Mode of Transport: </label>
  <select id="selectTransport" data-bind="ojComponent:
   {component: 'ojSelect', value: selectedVal,
    rootAttributes: {style:'max-width:20em'}}">
    <option value="W">Walk</option>
    <option value="B">Bicycle</option>
    <option value="M">Motor Cycle</option>
    <option value="C">Car</option>
    <option value="P">Public Transport</option>
  </select>
  <div>
    <br/> <hr/>
    <label for="selectedTransport">Selected Transport value is
    </label>
    <span id="selectedTransport"
          data-bind="text: ko.toJSON(selectedVal)"></span>
  </div>
</form>
```

- **JavaScript (single select)**:

```
require(['ojs/ojcore', 'knockout', 'jquery', 'ojs/ojknockout',
         'ojs/ojselectcombobox'],
function(oj, ko, $)
{
  $(function()
  {
    function ValueModel() {
```

```
                this.selectedVal = ko.observableArray(["C"]);
            }
            ko.applyBindings(new ValueModel(),
                            document.getElementById('form1'));
        });
    });
```

The output should be displayed on the page as follows:

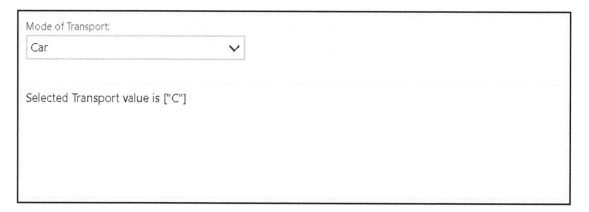

You can change the value of the select field (`Mode of Transport`) and see the label value underneath changing simultaneously as the two-way data binding is enabled. Additionally, it supports place holder, item with image, setting the component width, show as disabled field, and trigger events on selecting values.

The following is the example for the multi select component:

- **HTML (multi select)**:

```
<form id="form1">
  <label for="selectTransport">Mode of Transport: </label>
  <select id="selectTransport" data-bind="ojComponent:
   {component: 'ojSelect', value: selectedVal, multiple:true,
    rootAttributes: {style:'max-width:20em'}}">
    <option value="Walk">Walk</option>
    <option value="Bicycle">Bicycle</option>
    <option value="Motor Cycle">Motor Cycle</option>
    <option value="Car">Car</option>
    <option value="Public Transport">Public Transport</option>
  </select>
  <div>
    <br/> <hr/>
    <label for="selectedTransport">Selected Transport value is
```

```
      </label>
      <span id="selectedTransport"
            data-bind="text: ko.toJSON(selectedVal)"></span>
   </div>
</form>
```

- **JavaScript (multi select)**:

```
require(['ojs/ojcore', 'knockout', 'jquery', 'ojs/ojknockout',
         'ojs/ojselectcombobox'],
function(oj, ko, $)
{
   $(function()
   {
      function ValueModel() {
         this.selectedVal = ko.observableArray(["Bicycle","Car"]);
      }
      ko.applyBindings(new ValueModel(),
                       document.getElementById('form1'))
   });
});
```

The output should be displayed on the page as follows:

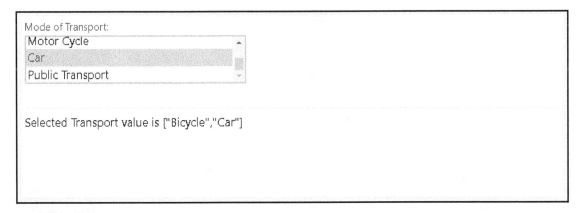

You can change the values of the multi select field (Mode of Transport) and see the label values changing simultaneously as the two-way data binding is enabled. Additionally, it supports place holder, item with image, setting the component width, show as disabled field, for each component, options binding, and trigger events on selecting values.

Combo box

The combo box is the element in which the values get populated in the element as we type. Create an `ojCombobox` component using the `ojComponent` binding with an ID. It enhances the HTML input and datalist components. To review the value of the combo box element, create an HTML label with the `for` attribute referring to the value of the ID from `ojCombobox`. Populate the value from the model layer.

The combo box component is available in two modes, single select and multi select. Let's look at examples for both. The following is the example for the single combo box component:

- **HTML (single combo box):**

```
<form id="form1">
  <label for="selectTransport">Mode of Transport: </label>
  <select id="selectTransport" data-bind="ojComponent:
   {component: 'ojCombobox', value: selectedVal,
    rootAttributes: {style:'max-width:20em'}}">
  <option>Walk</option>
  <option>Bicycle</option>
  <option>Motor Cycle</option>
  <option>Car</option>
  <option>Public Transport</option>
 </select>
 <div>
   <br/> <hr/>
   <label for="selectedTransport">Selected Transport value is
   </label>
   <span id="selectedTransport"
        data-bind="text: ko.toJSON(selectedVal)"></span>
 </div>
</form>
```

- **JavaScript (single combo box):**

```
require(['ojs/ojcore', 'knockout', 'jquery', 'ojs/ojknockout',
        'ojs/ojselectcombobox'],
function(oj, ko, $)
{
  $(function()
  {
    function ValueModel() {
      this.selectedVal = ko.observableArray(["Bicycle"]);
    }
    ko.applyBindings(new ValueModel(),
                    document.getElementById('form1'));
```

```
    });
  });
```

The output should be displayed on the page as follows:

You can change the value of the combo box field (`Mode of Transport`) by selecting or typing the value and watching the label value changing simultaneously as the two-way data binding is enabled. Additionally, it supports place holder, item with image, setting the component width, show as disabled field, and trigger events on selecting values.

The following is the example for the multi combo box component:

- **HTML (multi combo box):**

```
<form id="form1">
  <label for="selectTransport">Mode of Transport: </label>
  <select id="selectTransport" data-bind="ojComponent:
   {component: 'ojCombobox', value: selectedVal, multiple:true,
    rootAttributes: {style:'max-width:20em'}}">
    <option >Walk</option>
    <option >Bicycle</option>
    <option >Motor Cycle</option>
    <option >Car</option>
    <option >Public Transport</option>
  </select>
  <div>
    <br/><br/> <hr/><br/><br/>
    <label for="selectedTransport">Selected Transport value is
    </label>
    <span id="selectedTransport"
          data-bind="text: ko.toJSON(selectedVal)"></span>
  </div>
</form>
```

```
        </form>
```

- **JavaScript (multi combo box):**

```
        require(['ojs/ojcore', 'knockout', 'jquery', 'ojs/ojknockout',
                    'ojs/ojselectcombobox'],
        function(oj, ko, $)
        {
          $(function()
          {
            function ValueModel() {
                this.selectedVal = ko.observableArray(["Bicycle","Car"]);
            }
            ko.applyBindings(new ValueModel(),
                            document.getElementById('form1'));
          });
        });
```

The output should be displayed on the page as follows:

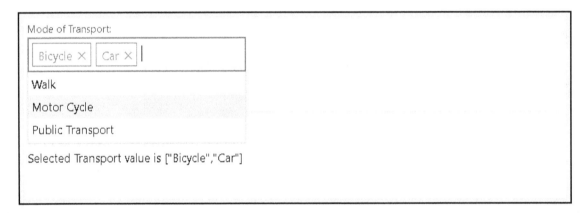

You can change the values of the multi combo box field (Mode of Transport) and see the label values changing simultaneously as the two-way data binding is enabled. Additionally, it supports place holder, item with image, setting the component width, show as disabled field, for each component, options binding, and trigger events on selecting values.

Checkbox set

Create an ojCheckboxset component using the ojComponent binding with an ID. To review the value of the checkbox element, create an HTML label with the for attribute referring to the value of the ID from ojCheckboxset. Populate the value from the model layer.

The checkbox component is available in two modes, single select and multi select.

The following is the example for both single and multi checkbox set components:

- **HTML:**

```
<form id="formId" class="oj-form">
  <label id="applyChanges">Apply Changes? </label>
  <div id="checkboxSetApplyChanges"
   aria-labelledby = "applyChanges"
   data-bind="ojComponent: { component: 'ojCheckboxset',
   value: applyChg, required:true}" >
    <!-- oj-choice-item is required for the component to work -->
    <span class="oj-choice-item">
      <input id="applyId" type="checkbox" value="apply">
      <label for="applyId">Apply</label>
    </span>
</div>
<br/>
<span>Apply Changes value is: </span>
<span id="curr-value" data-bind="text: applyChg"></span>
<br/>
<br/>
<br/>
<label id="mainlabelid">Browsers</label>
<!-- You need to set the aria-labelledby attribute
 to make this accessible.
 role="group" is set for you by ojCheckboxset. -->
<div id="checkboxSetId" aria-labelledby="mainlabelid"
 data-bind="ojComponent: { component: 'ojCheckboxset',
                           value: currentBrowser}" >
  <!-- oj-choice-item is required for the component to work -->
  <span class="oj-choice-item">
    <input id="ieopt" type="checkbox" value="Internet Explorer">
    <label for="ieopt">Internet Explorer</label>
  </span>
  <span class="oj-choice-item">
    <input id="chromeopt" type="checkbox" value="Chrome">
    <label for="chromeopt">Chrome</label>
  </span>
  <span class="oj-choice-item">
    <input id="firefoxopt" type="checkbox" value="Firefox">
    <label for="firefoxopt">Firefox</label>
  </span>
  <span class="oj-choice-item">
    <input id="operaopt" type="checkbox" value="Opera">
    <label for="Operaopt">Opera</label>
  </span>
```

```
    </div>
    <br/>
    <span>Current Browser value is: </span>
    <span id="curr-value" data-bind="text: currentBrowser"></span>
    <br/>
    <br/>
    <div id='buttons-container'>
      <a href="description.html"></a>
      <input id="inputButton3" type="button"
       data-bind=" click: setModelCurrentBrowser,
       ojComponent: {component: 'ojButton',
       label: 'Set currentBrowser to Chrome, Opera'}"/><br/>
    </div>
    </form>
```

- **JavaScript**:

```
require(['ojs/ojcore', 'knockout', 'jquery', 'ojs/ojknockout',
         'ojs/ojbutton', 'ojs/ojcheckboxset'],
function(oj, ko, $)
{
  function checkboxsetModel()
  {
    var self = this;
    // this variable keeps track of the currentBrowser.
    // It's a Knockout observable which means it is a two-way
binding.
    self.currentBrowser = ko.observableArray(["Firefox"]);
    self.applyChg = ko.observableArray();
    self.setModelCurrentBrowser = function() {
      self.currentBrowser(["Chrome", "Opera"]);
      return true;
    }
  }
  var vm = new checkboxsetModel();
  $(function()
  {
    ko.applyBindings(vm, document.getElementById('formId'));
  });
});
```

The output should be displayed on the page as follows. You can select the single checkbox or click on the button to change the values of the browsers:

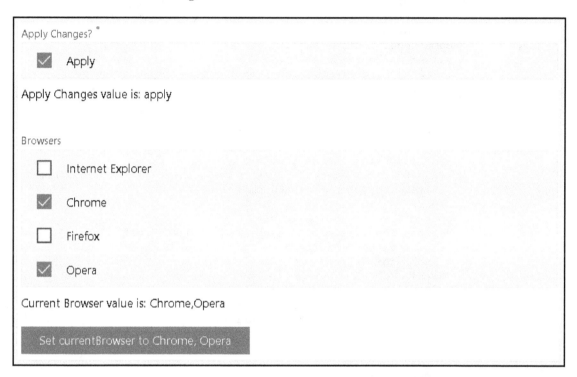

You can also change the value of the checkbox set by selecting each individual item and see the label value changing simultaneously as the two-way data binding is enabled. Additionally, it supports validation, group label, positioning the checkboxes, and trigger events on selecting values.

Radio set

Create an `ojRadioset` component using the `ojComponent` binding with an ID. To review the value of the radio box element, create an HTML label with the `for` attribute referring to the value of the ID from `ojRadioset`. Populate the value from the model layer.
The following is the example for the radio set component selection:

- **HTML:**

```
<form id="formId" class="oj-form">
    <label id="mainlabelid">Browsers</label>
```

```
<!-- You need to set the aria-labelledby attribute
 to make this accessible.
 role="radiogroup" is set for you by ojRadioset. -->
<div id="radiosetBasicDemoId" aria-labelledby="mainlabelid"
 data-bind="ojComponent: {
   component: 'ojRadioset',
   value: currentBrowser}" >
 <!-- oj-choice-item is required for the component to work -->
 <span class="oj-choice-item">
   <input id="ieopt" type="radio" name="icf"
          value="Internet Explorer">
   <label for="ieopt">Internet Explorer</label>
 </span>
 <span class="oj-choice-item">
   <input id="chromeopt" type="radio" name="icf" value="Chrome">
   <label for="chromeopt">Chrome</label>
 </span>
 <span class="oj-choice-item">
   <input id="firefoxopt" type="radio" name="icf"
          value="Firefox">
   <label for="firefoxopt">Firefox</label>
 </span>
 <span class="oj-choice-item">
   <input id="operaopt" type="radio" name="icf" value="Opera">
   <label for="operaopt">Opera</label>
 </span>
</div>
<br/>
<span>Current browser value is: </span>
<span id="curr-value" data-bind="text: currentBrowser"></span>
<br/>
<br/>
<div id='buttons-container'>
  <input id="inputButton4" type="button"
   data-bind="click: setModelCurrentBrowser,
   ojComponent: {
     component: 'ojButton',
     label: 'Set model currentBrowser to chrome'}"/><br/>
</div>
</form>
```

- **JavaScript**:

```
require(['ojs/ojcore', 'knockout', 'jquery', 'ojs/ojknockout',
         'ojs/ojradioset', 'ojs/ojbutton'],
function(oj, ko, $)
{
  function radiosetModel()
```

```
      {
        var self = this;
        // this variable keeps track of the currentBrowser.
        // It's a Knockout observable which means it is a two-way
binding.
        self.currentBrowser = ko.observable("Firefox");
        self.setModelCurrentBrowser = function() {
          alert("Set model currentBrowser to Chrome.");
          self.currentBrowser("Chrome");
          return true;
        }
      }
      var vm = new radiosetModel();
      $(function()
      {
        ko.applyBindings(vm, document.getElementById('formId'));
      });
    });
```

The output should be displayed on the page as follows. You can select the radio box or click on the button to change the values of the browsers:

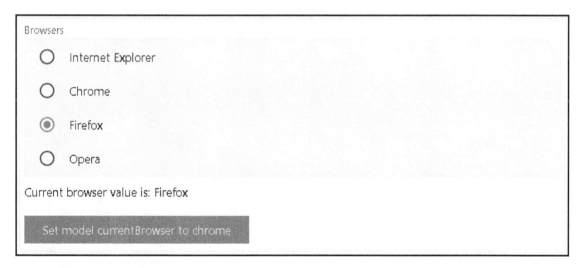

You can change the value of the radio box set and see the label value changing simultaneously as the two-way data binding is enabled. Additionally, it supports validation, context menu, positioning the radio boxes, and can be disabled.

Switch

Create an `ojSwitch` component using the `ojComponent` binding with an ID. To review the value of the switch element, create an HTML label with the `for` attribute referring to the value of the ID from `ojSwitch`. Populate the value from the model layer.

The following is the example for the switch component selection:

- **HTML:**

```
<form id="formId">
  <label id="switchLabel" for="status">Employment Status</label>
  <input id="status" data-bind="ojComponent: {component:
   'ojSwitch', value: isChecked}"/>
  <br/><br/>
  <span> Employment Status is </span>
  <span data-bind="text: ((isChecked()) ? 'Active' : 'Inactive')">
  </span>
</form>
```

- **JavaScript:**

```
require(['ojs/ojcore', 'knockout', 'jquery', 'ojs/ojknockout',
         'ojs/ojswitch'],
function(oj, ko, $)
{
  function SwitchModel(){
    this.isChecked = ko.observable();
  }
  var switchModel = new SwitchModel();
  $(function()
  {
    ko.applyBindings(switchModel,
        document.getElementById('formId'));
  });
});
```

The output should be displayed on the page as follows:

You can change the value of the switch element and see the label value changing simultaneously as the two-way data binding is enabled. Additionally, it supports ready only, disabled, and custom validation.

Form controls

Form controls are the components that help us indicate that one or more elements in the page are controlled to edit, read only, or disabled. When the form controls are disabled, you can't enter data into those components, whereas when they are enabled by the control components, you can go ahead and edit the data in the other fields.

The following example demonstrates the three states – Enabled, Disabled, and ReadOnly for the form components:

- **HTML:**

```
<div id="form-container">
  <div>
    <h5>Set State</h5>
    <div class="oj-buttonset-width-auto"
     data-bind="ojComponent: { component: 'ojButtonset',
                               checked: formState}">
      <label for="enabled">Enabled</label>
      <input type="radio" name="formstate" value="enabled"
       id="enabled" data-bind="ojComponent: { component:
                                             'ojButton'}"/>
      <label for="disabled">Disabled</label>
      <input type="radio" name="formstate" value="disabled"
       id="disabled" data-bind="ojComponent: { component:
                                              'ojButton'}"/>
      <label for="readonly">Read Only*</label>
      <input type="radio" name="formstate" value="readonly"
       id="readonly" data-bind="ojComponent: { component:
                                             'ojButton'}"/>
```

```
        </div>
        <p class="oj-text-sm oj-margin-lg-bottom">*
        readonly not supported on radio, checkbox, combobox,
        select, slider, input search, color palette, or
        color spectrum</p>
</div>
<div class="oj-form-layout">
    <div class="oj-form oj-sm-odd-cols-12 oj-md-odd-cols-4
    oj-md-labels-inline" >
        <div class="oj-flex">
            <div class="oj-flex-item">
                <label for="inputcontrol">First Name:</label>
            </div>
            <div class="oj-flex-item">
                <input id="inputcontrol"
                placeholder="placeholder text"
                data-bind="ojComponent: {
                    component: 'ojInputText',
                    value: placeholder()? null : 'John',
                    messagesCustom: messages,
                    disabled: disableFormControls,
                    readOnly: readonlyFormControls}">
            </div>
        </div>
        <div class="oj-flex">
            <div class="oj-flex-item">
                <label for="spinnercontrol">input number</label>
            </div>
            <div class="oj-flex-item">
                <input id="spinnercontrol"
                placeholder="placeholder text"
                data-bind="ojComponent: {
                    component: 'ojInputNumber',
                    messagesCustom: messages,
                    value: placeholder()? null : 20,
                    max:100, min:0, step:10,
                    disabled: disableFormControls,
                    readOnly: readonlyFormControls}"/>
            </div>
        </div>
        <div class="oj-flex">
            <div class="oj-flex-item">
                <label for="datetimepickercontrol">input datetime
                </label>
            </div>
            <div class="oj-flex-item">
                <input id="datetimepickercontrol"
                placeholder="placeholder text"
```

```
            data-bind="ojComponent: {
              component: 'ojInputDateTime',
              messagesCustom: messages,
              value: placeholder()? null :
              oj.IntlConverterUtils.dateToLocalIso(new Date()),
              disabled: disableFormControls,
              readOnly: readonlyFormControls}">
        </div>
      </div>
    </div>
  </div>
</div>
```

- **JavaScript:**

```
require(['ojs/ojcore', 'knockout', 'jquery',
    'ojs/ojknockout', 'ojs/ojinputtext', 'ojs/ojinputnumber',
    'ojs/ojdatetimepicker'],
function(oj, ko, $)
{
  function StateModel() {
    var self = this;
    self.formState = ko.observable('enabled');
    self.placeholder = ko.observable(false);
    self.disableFormControls = ko.computed(function () {
      if (self.formState() == 'disabled')
        return true;
      else
        return false;
    });
    self.readonlyFormControls = ko.computed(function () {
      if (self.formState() == 'readonly')
        return true;
      else
        return false;
    });
    self.messages = ko.observableArray([]);
  }
  $(function()
  {
    ko.applyBindings(new StateModel(),
        document.getElementById('form-container'));
  });
});
```

The output page should render the form controls in the following screenshot with the enabled state by default:

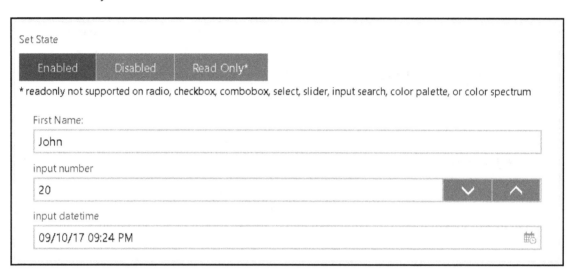

You can change the state of the input components with the help of the three-button combo (buttonset) on the top of the page. Click on the **Disabled** button to see all the form elements that have been disabled, as shown in the following screenshot:

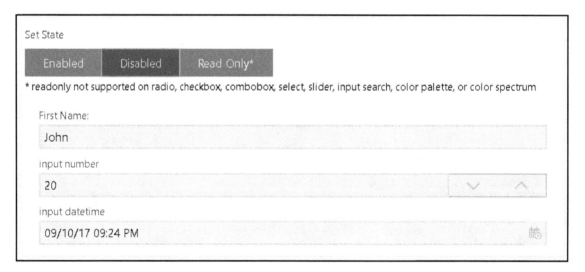

By clicking on the `Read Only*` button, you can see only the values corresponding to each of the input elements on the following form:

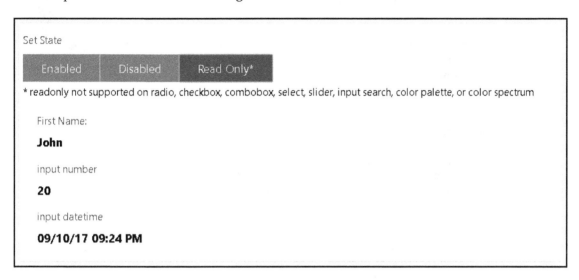

Through form controls, Oracle JET is allowing us to reuse the same form fields based on the attributes, and set their values based on the component state, and populate read only/disabled/editable form based on the requirement.

Data collections

Data collection components are the display components that let us easily populate the record of data in different elements, including `ojTable`, `ojDataGrid`, `ojTree`, and `ojListView`.

Each of the data collection components allows us to render the records along with additional options for auto layout, dynamic scrolling, column sorting, and pagination. Let's review `ojTable` with pagination in the following example:

- **HTML:**

```
<div id="pagingControlDemo">
  <table id="table" summary="Cities List"
  aria-label="Cities Table"
  data-bind="ojComponent: {component: 'ojTable',
    data: pagingDatasource, columns: [
      {headerText: 'Country', field: 'country'},
```

```
            {headerText: 'City Name', field: 'name'},
            {headerText: 'Lattitude', field: 'lat'},
            {headerText: 'Longitude', field: 'lng'}],
        rootAttributes: {'style':'width: 100%;'}}">
    </table>
    <div id="paging" data-bind="ojComponent: {
     component: 'ojPagingControl', data: pagingDatasource,
     pageSize: 10}">
    </div>
  </div>
```

- **JavaScript:**

```
require(['ojs/ojcore', 'knockout', 'jquery', 'ojs/ojknockout',
    'ojs/ojtable', 'ojs/ojpagingcontrol',
    'ojs/ojpagingtabledatasource', 'ojs/ojarraytabledatasource'],
    function(oj, ko, $)
    {
      function viewModel()
      {
        var self = this;
        var citiesArray = [
          { "country": "AD", "name": "Pas de la Casa",
            "lat": "42.54277", "lng": "1.73361" },
          { "country": "AD", "name": "Ordino", "lat": "42.55623",
            "lng": "1.53319" },
          { "country": "AD", "name": "les Escaldes",
            "lat": "42.50729", "lng": "1.53414" },
          { "country": "AD", "name": "la Massana",
            "lat": "42.54499", "lng": "1.51483" },
          { "country": "AD", "name": "Encamp", "lat": "42.53474",
            "lng": "1.58014" },
          { "country": "AD", "name": "Canillo", "lat": "42.5676",
            "lng": "1.59756" },
          { "country": "AE", "name": "Umm al Qaywayn",
            "lat": "25.56473", "lng": "55.55517" },
          { "country": "AE", "name": "Ras al-Khaimah",
            "lat": "25.78953", "lng": "55.9432" },
          { "country": "AE", "name": "Muzayri'",
            "lat": "23.14355", "lng": "53.7881" },
          { "country": "AE", "name": "Khawr Fakkān",
            "lat": "25.33132", "lng": "56.34199" },
          { "country": "US", "name": "Greensboro",
            "lat": "32.70415", "lng": "-87.5955" },
          { "country": "US", "name": "Greenville",
            "lat": "31.8296", "lng": "-86.61775" },
          { "country": "US", "name": "Grove Hill",
            "lat": "31.70877", "lng": "-87.77722" },
```

```
        { "country": "US", "name": "Guin", "lat": "33.96566",
          "lng": "-87.91475" },
        { "country": "US", "name": "Gulf Shores",
          "lat": "30.24604", "lng": "-87.70082" },
        { "country": "US", "name": "Guntersville",
          "lat": "34.35823", "lng": "-86.29446" },
        { "country": "US", "name": "Hackleburg",
          "lat": "34.27732", "lng": "-87.82864" },
        { "country": "US", "name": "Haleyville",
          "lat": "34.22649", "lng": "-87.62141" },
        { "country": "US", "name": "Hamilton",
          "lat": "34.14232", "lng": "-87.98864" },
        { "country": "US", "name": "Hanceville",
          "lat": "34.06065", "lng": "-86.7675" },
        { "country": "US", "name": "Harpersville",
          "lat": "33.344", "lng": "-86.43804" },
        { "country": "US", "name": "West Warrenton",
          "lat": "33.41217", "lng": "-82.67517" },
        { "country": "US", "name": "Johnston",
          "lat": "41.82186", "lng": "-71.50675" },
        { "country": "US", "name": "Hill Air Force Base",
          "lat": "41.11118", "lng": "-111.97712" },
        { "country": "US", "name": "Elmendorf Air Force Base",
          "lat": "61.25703", "lng": "-149.63139" },
        { "country": "US", "name": "Hot Springs National
          Park", "lat": "34.5317", "lng": "-93.06377" },
        { "country": "US", "name": "Dixiana",
          "lat": "33.74021", "lng": "-86.64938" },
        { "country": "US", "name": "Shoal Creek",
          "lat": "33.43076", "lng": "-86.61092" },
        { "country": "ZW", "name": "Binga",
          "lat": "-17.62027", "lng": "27.34139" },
        { "country": "ZW", "name": "Bindura",
          "lat": "-17.30192", "lng": "31.33056" },
        { "country": "ZW", "name": "Beitbridge",
          "lat": "-22.21667", "lng": "30" },
        { "country": "ZW", "name": "Beatrice",
          "lat": "-18.25283", "lng": "30.8473" },
        { "country": "ZW", "name": "Banket",
          "lat": "-17.38333", "lng": "30.4" },
        { "country": "ZW", "name": "Epworth", "lat": "-17.89",
          "lng": "31.1475" }
    ];
    self.pagingDatasource = new oj.PagingTableDataSource
        (new oj.ArrayTableDataSource(citiesArray,
            {idAttribute: 'name'}));
}
var vm = new viewModel;
```

```
$(document).ready(function()
{
  ko.applyBindings(vm, document
    .getElementById('pagingControlDemo'));
});
});
```

Serving the page populates the sortable cities table with pagination features, as shown in the following screenshot:

Country ▼	City Name	Lattitude	Longitude
ZW	Epworth	-17.89	31.1475
ZW	Banket	-17.38333	30.4
ZW	Beatrice	-18.25283	30.8473
ZW	Beitbridge	-22.21667	30
ZW	Bindura	-17.30192	31.33056
ZW	Binga	-17.62027	27.34139
US	Haleyville	34.22649	-87.62141
US	Shoal Creek	33.43076	-86.61092
US	Dixiana	33.74021	-86.64938
US	Hot Springs National Park	34.5317	-93.06377

Page 1 of 4 (1-10 of 34 items) K < | 1 | 2 3 4 > >|

We can sort the records, in an ascending or descending order, based on either of the columns by clicking on the header, we can navigate through the pages by clicking the page number or the next/end of record buttons, or we can navigate directly to the page we want by entering the page number in the Page field on the footer of the table.

Summary

In this chapter, we learned the rich Oracle JET components and steps involved in adding the components to web pages. We also learned about different form components offered by the Oracle JET frameworks. We finished this chapter with an understanding of how form controls and data collection components help control the form fields and populate large records of data on the applications.

In the next chapter, we will learn about the advanced Oracle JET components, including layouts, navigation, and visualizations.

6
OJ Components – Layouts, Navigation, and Visualizations

Components such as forms, controls, and data collection provide the basic needs of web application development with the Oracle JET framework, as discussed in the previous chapter. Modern web applications are expected to have visual grandeur in the way the application design and theme are presented along with the visualizations, layouts, and navigation. Oracle JET provides such components out of the box, and has made it way easier to use them with declarative components with bindings to the application state.

In this chapter, we will cover the following topics:

- Visualization components
- Layout and navigation components

Visualization components

Presentation of hierarchical data is an art. You can present it using a simple parent-child kind of tabular representation, as well as with visualization components such as charts and gauges that enhance the user experience of the way hierarchical data is presented. In this section, we will review the set of Oracle JET visualization components that help us present hierarchical data in the most presentable form.

The following are some of the key visualization components of the Oracle JET framework, along with the corresponding API provided by the framework:

Component Group	Component Name	Corresponding API
Charts	Area	ojChart
	Bar	
	Bubble	
	Combination	
	Funnel	
	Line	
	Line with Area	
	Pie	
	Polar	
	Range	
	Scatter	
	Spark	
	Stock	
Gauges	Dial	ojDialGauge
	LED	ojLEDGauge
	Rating	ojRatingGauge
	Status Meter	ojStatusMeterGauge
Other Visualization Components	Diagram	ojDiagram
	Legend	ojLegend
	NBox	ojNBox
	Sunburst	ojSunburst
	Tag Cloud	ojTagCloud
	Thematic Map	ojThematicMap
	Timeline	ojTimeLine
	Treemap	ojTreeMap

Charts

Charts are the basic visualization components for representing multidimensional data in a graphical illustration. Oracle JET lets us generate diverse chart types, from area to stock, using the `ojChart` component as listed in the previous section. Let us review a basic area chart example.

Area charts

Create an `ojChart` component using the type `area` binding with an ID. Provide different values for the groups and series with a default orientation of `horizontal`. The following is an example for an area chart:

- **HTML**:

```
<div id='chart-container'>
  <div id="areaChart" data-bind="ojComponent: {
    component: 'ojChart',
    type: 'area',
    series: areaSeriesValue,
    groups: areaGroupsValue,
    animationOnDisplay: 'auto',
    animationOnDataChange: 'auto',
    orientation: orientationValue,
    stack: stackValue,
    hoverBehavior: 'dim'
  }"
  style="max-width:500px;width:100%;height:350px;">
  </div>
  <div id="myToolbar" aria-label="Chart Display Options Toolbar"
   aria-controls="areaChart" data-bind="ojComponent:
   {component:'ojToolbar'}"
   style="max-width:500px;width:100%;">
     <!-- vertical/horizontal toggle button -->
     <div id="radioButtonset" data-bind="ojComponent:
      {component: 'ojButtonset',
      focusManagement:'none', checked: orientationValue,
      chroming: 'half'}" aria-label="Choose an orientation.">
       <!-- ko foreach: orientationOptions -->
       <label data-bind="attr: {for: id}"></label>
       <input type="radio" name="orientation"
        data-bind="value: value, attr: {id: id}, ojComponent:
        {component: 'ojButton', label: label,
         icons: {start: icon}, display: 'icons'}"/>
       <!-- /ko -->
     </div>
     <span role="separator" aria-orientation="vertical"
      class="oj-toolbar-separator"></span>
     <!-- unstacked/stacked toggle button -->
     <div id="radioButtonset2" data-bind="ojComponent:
      {component: 'ojButtonset', focusManagement:'none',
       checked: stackValue, chroming: 'half'}"
       aria-label="Choose a stack setting.">
       <!-- ko foreach: stackOptions -->
```

```
            <label data-bind="attr: {for: id}"></label>
            <input type="radio" name="stack"
             data-bind="value: value, attr: {id: id},
             ojComponent: {component: 'ojButton', label: label,
             icons: {start: icon}, display: 'icons'}"/>
            <!-- /ko -->
          </div>
        </div>
      </div>
```

- **JavaScript:**

```
require(['ojs/ojcore', 'knockout', 'jquery', 'ojs/ojknockout',
         'ojs/ojbutton', 'ojs/ojchart', 'ojs/ojtoolbar'],
function(oj, ko, $)
{
  function ChartModel() {
    var self = this;
     /* toggle button variables */
    self.stackValue = ko.observable('off');
    self.orientationValue = ko.observable('vertical');
     /* chart data */
    var areaSeries = [{name : "Series A",
                        items : [74, 42, 70, 46]},
                       {name : "Series B",
                        items : [50, 38, 46, 54]},
                       {name : "Series C",
                        items : [34, 22, 30, 32]},
                       {name : "Series D",
                        items : [18, 16, 4, 22]}];
    var areaGroups = ["Group 1", "Group 2", "Group 3",
                       "Group 4"];
    this.areaSeriesValue = ko.observableArray(areaSeries);
    this.areaGroupsValue = ko.observableArray(areaGroups);
     /* toggle buttons*/
    self.stackOptions = [
      {id: 'unstacked', label: 'unstacked', value: 'off',
       icon: 'oj-icon demo-area-vert'},
      {id: 'stacked', label: 'stacked', value: 'on',
       icon: 'oj-icon demo-area-stack'}
    ];
    self.orientationOptions = [
      {id: 'vertical', label: 'vertical', value: 'vertical',
       icon: 'oj-icon demo-area-vert'},
      {id: 'horizontal', label: 'horizontal',
       value: 'horizontal', icon: 'oj-icon demo-area-horiz'}
    ];
  }
```

```
var chartModel = new ChartModel();
$(function()
{
  ko.applyBindings(chartModel,
      document.getElementById('chart-container'));
});
});
```

The output should be displayed in the page:

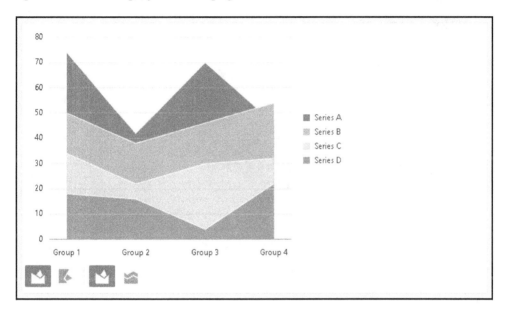

You can change the orientation to horizontal and stacked options by clicking on the icons below the chart. Additionally, it supports animations, hide/show, different line types (straight/curved stepped/centered stepped), and different styles.

Gauges

Gauges let us represent a metric value in the range of min. to max. value specified on the element. Oracle JET provides various gauge components, and the following are the types of gauges:

- Dial
- LED

- Rating
- Status meter

Dial gauges

Dial gauge components can be populated by adding an `ojDialGauge` element, setting the value to be set on the gauge. Following code snippet is for the dial guage:

- **HTML:**

```
<div id='gauge-container'>
  <div id="gauge1"
   data-bind="ojComponent: {
     component: 'ojDialGauge',
     value: gaugeValue,
     readOnly: false,
     animationOnDisplay: 'auto',
     indicator: 'needleAlta',
     background: 'circleAlta',
     metricLabel: {rendered: 'on',
     style: 'font-size: 18px; font-weight: bold;
        font-family: Georgia, Times New Roman, serif;'}
   }"
   style="width:250px;height:250px">
  </div>
</div>
```

- **JavaScript:**

```
require(['ojs/ojcore', 'knockout', 'jquery', 'ojs/ojknockout',
         'ojs/ojgauge'],
function(oj, ko, $)
{
  function dialGaugeData() {
    this.gaugeValue = ko.observable(65);
  }
  $(function()
  {
    ko.applyBindings(new dialGaugeData(),
       document.getElementById('gauge-container'));
  });
});
```

The output should be displayed in the page:

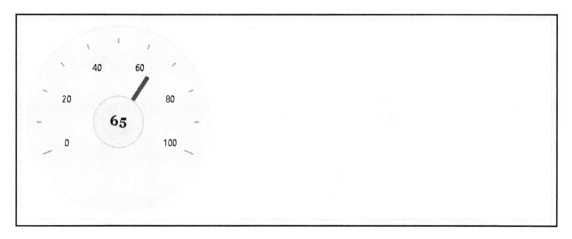

LED gauges

LED gauges help in representing components with various metric values to be highlighted in the element. They are available in different types of elements, such as circle, arrow, diamond, rectangle, star, or triangle. They can be added with the element `ojLedGauge` as shown in the following example, where we see LED gauges in different colors, in a range of values:

- **HTML:**

```
<div id="ledContent" style="height:100%; width: 100%;
position:relative;">
  <svg height="0" width="0">
    <defs>
      <pattern id="pattern"
       width="3" height="3"
       patternUnits="userSpaceOnUse"
       patternTransform="rotate(45)">
        <rect width="3" height="3" fill="#336791"></rect>
        <rect x="1.5" width="3" height="3" fill="#ADD8E6" ></rect>
      </pattern>
    </defs>
  </svg>
  <table>
    <tr>
      <td>
        <label>Thresholds:</label>
```

```
      </td>
      <td>
        <div title="25 (Low)" style="float: left; width:40px;
         height:40px;" data-bind="ojComponent: {
           component: 'ojLedGauge',
           min: 0,
           max: 100,
           thresholds: thresholdValues,
           metricLabel: {rendered: 'on'},
           value: lowValue}"></div>
        <div title="50 (Medium)" style="float: left;
         width:40px; height:40px;" data-bind="ojComponent: {
           component: 'ojLedGauge',
           min: 0, max: 100,
           thresholds: thresholdValues,
           metricLabel: {rendered: 'on'},
           value: midValue}"></div>
        <div title="75 (High)" style="float: left; width:40px;
         height:40px;" data-bind="ojComponent: {
           component: 'ojLedGauge',
           min: 0,
           max: 100,
           thresholds: thresholdValues,
           metricLabel: {rendered: 'on'},
           value: highValue}"></div>
      </td>
    </tr>
  </table>
</div>
```

- **JavaScript:**

```
require(['ojs/ojcore', 'knockout', 'jquery', 'ojs/ojknockout',
        'ojs/ojgauge'],
function(oj, ko, $)
{
  function ViewModel() {
    this.lowValue = ko.observable(25);
    this.midValue = ko.observable(50);
    this.highValue = ko.observable(75);
    this.thresholdValues = [{max: 33}, {max: 67}, {}];
  }
  $(function()
  {
    ko.applyBindings(new ViewModel(),
       document.getElementById('ledContent'));
  });
});
```

The output should be displayed in the page:

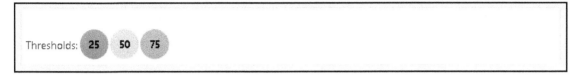

This component can also be displayed in different shapes and directions as desired.

Rating gauges

Rating gauges are used to represent the feedback rating of an object through the metric value over a scale. An `ojRatingGauge` component can be added with a value, and is available in different shapes, colors, directions, and states. The following example shows the standard rating gauge representation:

- **HTML:**

```
<div id='gauge-container'>
  <svg height="0" width="0">
    <defs>
      <pattern id="pattern"
       width="3" height="3"
       patternUnits="userSpaceOnUse"
       patternTransform="rotate(45)">
        <rect width="3" height="3" fill="#336791"></rect>
        <rect x="1.5" width="3" height="3" fill="#ADD8E6" ></rect>
      </pattern>
      <pattern id="hoverPattern"
       width="3" height="3"
       patternUnits="userSpaceOnUse"
       patternTransform="rotate(45)">
        <rect width="3" height="3" fill="red"></rect>
        <rect x="1.5" width="3" height="3" fill="#ADD8E6" ></rect>
      </pattern>
    </defs>
  </svg>
  <table>
    <tr>
      <td>
        <label> Editable:</label>
      </td>
      <td>
        <div id="gauge2" data-bind="ojComponent: {
          component: 'ojRatingGauge',
```

```
                value:ratingValue2,
                readOnly: false
            }"
            style="width:120px;height:25px">
          </div>
        </td>
      </tr>
    </table>
  </div>
```

- **JavaScript:**

```
require(['ojs/ojcore', 'knockout', 'jquery', 'ojs/ojknockout',
         'ojs/ojgauge'],
function(oj, ko, $)
{
  this.gaugeValue = ko.observable(3);
  function ratingGaugeData() {
    this.ratingValue2 = ko.observable(3);
    this.rawValue = ko.observable();
    this.thresholdValues = [{max: 1, shortDesc: 'Poor'},
                {max: 2, shortDesc: 'Needs Improvement'},
                {max: 3, shortDesc: 'Satisfactory'},
                {max: 4, shortDesc: 'Exceeds Expectations'},
                {max: 5, shortDesc: 'Outstanding'}];
    this.optionChangeAction = function(e, data) {
      if(data.option == "value") {
        ratingGaugeModel.ratingValue10 = data['value'];
        $('#currentStepText').html("optionChange: " +
           ko.toJSON(data['value']));
        $('#currentStepText').css('color', 'Green');
      }
    }
  }
  var ratingGaugeModel = new ratingGaugeData();
  $(function()
  {
    ko.applyBindings(ratingGaugeModel,
       document.getElementById('gauge-container'));
  });
});
```

The output should be displayed in the page:

Editable: ★ ★ ★ ★ ★

The component can be associated with event listeners to trigger any behavior on changing the value of the rating gauge.

Status meter gauges

Status meter gauges represent the current element status in different directions. The component can be represented in horizontal, vertical, circular, and center content models. `ojStatusMeterGauge` can be used with the orientation to represent this element. Create an `ojInputPassword` component using the `ojComponent` binding with an ID. To review the value of a `password` element, create an HTML label with attributes referring to the value of ID from `ojInputPassword`. Populate the value from the model layer:

- **HTML:**

```
<div id='gauge-container'>
  <table>
    <tr>
      <td>
        <label>Reference Lines:</label>
      </td>
      <td style="width:200px;">
        <div id="gauge" title="Value: 20<br>
         Reference Lines: Low 33, Medium 67, High 100"
         data-bind="ojComponent: {
           component: 'ojStatusMeterGauge',
           min: 0,
           max: 100,
           value: value1,
           orientation: 'circular',
           optionChange: gaugeOptionChange,
           metricLabel: {rendered: 'on'},
           plotArea: {rendered: 'on'},
           referenceLines:
           [{value: 33, color:'red'},
            {value: 67, color:'green'}],
           indicatorSize: 0.5,
           readOnly: false
         }"
```

```
                          style= "align:center;
                          margin-top:5px;
                          margin-bottom:5px;
                          height:50px;
                          width:45%;">
                        </div>
                      </td>
                    </tr>
                    <tr>
                      <td>
                        <label>Start Angle and Angle Extent:</label>
                      </td>
                      <td>
                        <div id="gauge8" data-bind="ojComponent: {
                          component: 'ojStatusMeterGauge',
                          min: 0,
                          max: 100,
                          value: value2,
                          orientation: 'circular',
                          startAngle:180,
                          angleExtent: 180,
                          metricLabel: {rendered: 'on'},
                          plotArea: {rendered: 'on'},
                          readOnly: false
                        }"
                        style= "align:center;
                        margin-top:5px;
                        margin-bottom:5px;
                        height:50px;
                        width:45%; ">
                        </div>
                      </td>
                    </tr>
                  </table>
                </div>
```

- **JavaScript:**

```
require(['ojs/ojcore', 'knockout', 'jquery', 'ojs/ojknockout',
         'ojs/ojgauge'],
function(oj, ko, $)
{
  function statusmeterGaugeData() {
    this.value1 = ko.observable(20);
    this.value2 = ko.observable(80);
    this.thresholdValues = [{max: 33}, {max: 67}, {}];
    var converterFactory = oj.Validation
                             .converterFactory('number');
```

```
        var currencyConverter = converterFactory
            .createConverter({style: 'currency', currency: 'USD'});
        this.valueConverter = ko.observable(currencyConverter);
        this.gaugeOptionChange = function(e, data) {
          if (data.option == "value") {
            $("#gauge").attr('title', "Value: " +
              Math.round(data['value']) + "<br>Reference Lines:
              Low 33, Medium 67, High 100");
            $("#gauge").ojStatusMeterGauge('refresh');
          }
        }
      }
    var statusmeterGaugeModel = new statusmeterGaugeData();
    $(function()
    {
      ko.applyBindings(statusmeterGaugeModel,
        document.getElementById('gauge-container'));
    });
  });
```

The output should be displayed in the page:

You can also review the tooltip values by hovering on the element. Each dimension and color can also be changed as per the requirement.

Trendy visualization components

Oracle JET has a few trendy visualization components as well, namely Diagram, Legend, NBox, Sunburst, Tag Cloud, Thematic Map, Timeline, and Treemap.

Sunbursts

Sunbursts are a visual representation of two-dimensional hierarchical information in a circular model. Data is represented in size and color distinct from others based on their value. In the following example, the sunburst component is plotted using `ojSunburst` with the nodes assigned with data values:

- **HTML:**

```
<div id='sunburst-container'>
  <div data-bind="ojComponent: {
     component: 'ojSunburst',
     animationOnDisplay: 'auto',
     sizeLabel: 'Population',
     colorLabel: 'Median Household Income',
     nodeDefaults: {labelDisplay: 'rotated'},
     nodes: nodeValues
   }"
   style="max-width:750px;width:100%; height:750px;">
  </div>
</div>
```

- **JavaScript:**

```
require(['ojs/ojcore', 'knockout', 'jquery', 'ojs/ojknockout',
         'ojs/ojsunburst'],
function(oj, ko, $)
{
  var handler = new oj.ColorAttributeGroupHandler();
  var unitedStates = createNode("United States", 301461533, 51425);
  var reg_NE = createNode("Northeast Region", 54906297, 57208);
  var reg_MW = createNode("Midwest Region", 66336038, 49932);
  var reg_SO = createNode("South Region", 110450832, 47204);
  var reg_WE = createNode("West Region", 69768366, 56171);

  var div_NE = createNode("New England", 14315257, 61511);
  var div_MA = createNode("Middle Atlantic", 40591040, 55726);
  var div_EN = createNode("East North Central", 46277998, 50156);
  var div_WN = createNode("West North Central", 20058040, 49443);
  var div_SA = createNode("South Atlantic", 57805475, 50188);
  var div_ES = createNode("East South Central", 17966553, 41130);
var div_WS = createNode("West South Central", 34678804, 45608);
var div_MO = createNode("Mountain", 21303294, 51504);
var div_PA = createNode("Pacific", 48465072, 58735);
addChildNodes(unitedStates, [reg_NE, reg_MW, reg_SO, reg_WE]);
addChildNodes(reg_NE, [div_NE, div_MA]);
addChildNodes(reg_MW, [div_EN, div_WN]);
```

```
addChildNodes(reg_SO, [div_SA, div_ES, div_WS]);
addChildNodes(reg_WE, [div_MO, div_PA]);
addChildNodes(div_NE, [
  createNode("Connecticut", 3494487, 67721),
  createNode("Maine", 1316380, 46541),
  createNode("Massachusetts", 6511176, 64496),
  createNode("New Hampshire", 1315419, 63033),
  createNode("Rhode Island", 1057381, 55569),
  createNode("Vermont", 620414, 51284)
]);
addChildNodes(div_MA, [
  createNode("New Jersey", 8650548, 68981),
  createNode("New York", 19423896, 55233),
  createNode("Pennsylvania", 12516596, 49737)
]);
addChildNodes(div_EN, [
  createNode("Indiana", 6342469, 47465),
  createNode("Illinois", 12785043, 55222),
  createNode("Michigan", 10039208, 48700),
  createNode("Ohio", 11511858, 47144),
  createNode("Wisconsin", 5599420, 51569)
]);
addChildNodes(div_WN, [
  createNode("Iowa", 2978880, 48052),
  createNode("Kansas", 2777835, 48394),
  createNode("Minnesota", 5188581, 57007),
  createNode("Missouri", 5904382, 46005),
  createNode("Nebraska", 1772124, 47995),
  createNode("North Dakota", 639725, 45140),
  createNode("South Dakota", 796513, 44828)
]);
addChildNodes(div_SA, [
  createNode("Delaware", 863832, 57618),
  createNode("District of Columbia", 588433, 56519),
  createNode("Florida", 18222420, 47450),
  createNode("Georgia", 9497667, 49466),
  createNode("Maryland", 5637418, 69475),
  createNode("North Carolina", 9045705, 45069),
  createNode("South Carolina", 4416867, 43572),
  createNode("Virginia", 7721730, 60316),
  createNode("West Virginia", 1811403, 37356)
]);
addChildNodes(div_ES, [
  createNode("Alabama", 4633360, 41216),
  createNode("Kentucky", 4252000, 41197),
  createNode("Mississippi", 2922240, 36796),
  createNode("Tennessee", 6158953, 42943)
]);
```

```
addChildNodes(div_WS, [
  createNode("Arkansas", 2838143, 38542),
  createNode("Louisiana", 4411546, 42167),
  createNode("Oklahoma", 3610073, 41861),
  createNode("Texas", 23819042, 48199)
]);
addChildNodes(div_MO, [
  createNode("Arizona", 6324865, 50296),
  createNode("Colorado", 4843211, 56222),
  createNode("Idaho", 1492573, 46183),
  createNode("Montana", 956257, 43089),
  createNode("Nevada", 2545763, 55585),
  createNode("New Mexico", 1964860, 42742),
  createNode("Utah", 2651816, 55642),
  createNode("Wyoming", 523949, 51990)
]);
addChildNodes(div_PA, [
  createNode("Alaska", 683142, 64635),
  createNode("California", 36308527, 60392),
  createNode("Hawaii", 1280241, 64661),
  createNode("Oregon", 3727407, 49033),
  createNode("Washington", 6465755, 56384)
]);
function createNode(label, population, meanIncome) {
  return {label: label,
          id: label,
          value: population,
          color: getColor(meanIncome),
          shortDesc: "&lt;b&gt;" + label +
          "&lt;/b&gt;&lt;br/&gt;Population: " +
          population+"&lt;br/&gt;Income: " + meanIncome};
  }
  function getColor(meanIncome) {
    if (meanIncome < 45000) // 1st quartile
      return handler.getValue('1stQuartile');
    else if (meanIncome < 49000) // 2nd quartile
      return handler.getValue('2ndQuartile');
    else if (meanIncome < 56000) // 3rd quartile
      return handler.getValue('3rdQuartile');
    else
      return handler.getValue('4thQuartile');
  }
  function addChildNodes(parent, childNodes) {
    parent.nodes = [];
    for (var i = 0; i < childNodes.length; i++) {
      parent.nodes.push(childNodes[i]);
    }
  }
```

```
$(function()
{
  ko.applyBindings({nodeValues:
    ko.observableArray([unitedStates])},
  document.getElementById('sunburst-container'));
});
});
```

The output should be displayed in the page:

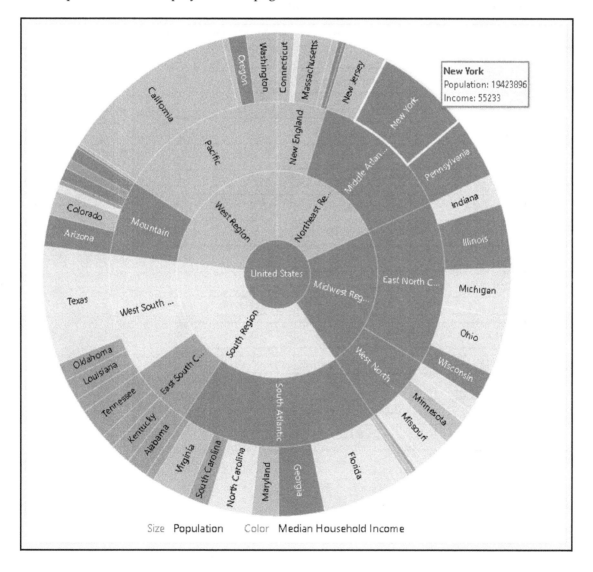

You can also review the tooltip values by hovering on the element. These components support animations, drilling, adding legends, popups, and tooltip customizations.

Layout and navigation components

Oracle JET enhances the HTML components with additional attributes, patterns, and components to provide the layout and navigation for applications.

The following are some of the key layout and navigation components of the Oracle JET framework, along with the corresponding API provided by the framework:

Sr. no.	Component name	Corresponding API
1	Accordion	`ojAccordion`
2	Collapsible	`ojCollapsible`
3	Conveyor belt	`ojConveyorBelt`
4	Dialog	`ojDialog`
5	Film strip	`ojFilmStrip`
6	HTML tags	Heading, HR, link, list, and paragraph
7	Masonry layout	`ojMasonryLayout`
8	Navigation list	`ojNavigationList`
9	offCanvas utils	`offCanvasUtils`
10	Panel	`ojpanel-*`
11	Popup	`ojPopup`
12	Progress indicator	`ojProgressbar`
13	Tab	`ojTabs`
14	Train	`ojTrain`

Layout and navigation examples

Let us review the examples for some of these layout and navigation components in this section.

Accordions

An accordion element lets the collapsible element contain multiple subelements to choose the options. An `ojAccordion` element can be added with the subelements of collapsible and other HTML elements:

- **HTML:**

```
<div id="accordionPage" data-bind="ojComponent: {component:
'ojAccordion'}">
  <div id="c3" data-bind="ojComponent: {component:
  'ojCollapsible', expanded:true}">
   <span>Header 1</span>
   <div>
     <label id="mainlabelid">Vehicle of your Choice</label>
       <div id="radiosetSetBasicDemoId"
         aria-labelledby= "mainlabelid" data-bind="ojComponent:
         {component: 'ojRadioset', value: 'car'}" >
         <span class="oj-choice-item">
           <input id="bikeopt" type="radio"
           name="vehicle" value="bike">
           <label for="bikeopt">Bike</label>
         </span>
         <span class="oj-choice-item">
           <input id="caropt" type="radio"
           name="vehicle" value="car">
           <label for="caropt">Car</label>
         </span>
         <span class="oj-choice-item">
           <input id="planeopt" type="radio"
           name="vehicle" value="plane">
           <label for="planeopt">Plane</label>
         </span>
       </div>
     </div>
   </div>
   <div id="c4">
     <span>Header 2</span>
     <div id="nestedAccordion" data-bind= "ojComponent:
     {component: 'ojAccordion'}" >
       <div id="ic1">
```

```
              <span>Inner Header 2.1</span>
              <p class="oj-p">Inner Content of 2.1</p>
          </div>
          <div id="ic2" data-bind="ojComponent:
           {component: 'ojCollapsible'}">
             <span>Inner Header 2.2</span>
             <p class="oj-p">Inner Content of 2.2</p>
          </div>
        </div>
      </div>
    </div>
```

- **JavaScript:**

```
require(['ojs/ojcore', 'knockout', 'jquery', 'ojs/ojknockout',
      'ojs/ojaccordion', 'ojs/ojcollapsible', 'ojs/ojradioset'],
function(oj, ko, $)
{
  $(function()
  {
    ko.applyBindings(null,
    document.getElementById('accordionPage'))
  });
});
```

The output should be displayed in the page:

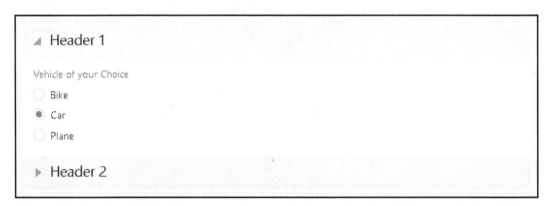

We can also have multiple expansions and event triggered on accordion selection.

Modal dialogs

A modal component helps with the user input through the overlay window which gives an intuitive visual effect instead of blocking popup windows. An `ojDialog` element can be added as per the requirement, it can present the input form and take user input and provide the response through the interface. The `OK` button confirms the choice, and applies the state to the variable:

- **HTML:**

```html
<div id="dialogWrapper">
  <div style="display:none" id="modalDialog1"
   title="Modal Dialog Title"
   data-bind="ojComponent:{component: 'ojDialog',
     initialVisibility: 'hide'}">
    <div class="oj-dialog-body">
      A movable, resizable and closable dialog window.
    </div>
    <div class="oj-dialog-footer">
      <button id="okButton" data-bind="ojComponent: {
        component: 'ojButton', label: 'OK'}"> </button>
    </div>
  </div>
  <button id="buttonOpener" data-bind="ojComponent: {
     component: 'ojButton', label: 'Open Dialog'}"></button>
</div>
```

- **JavaScript:**

```javascript
require(['ojs/ojcore', 'knockout', 'jquery', 'ojs/ojknockout',
        'ojs/ojbutton', 'ojs/ojdialog'],
function(oj, ko, $)
{
  function dialogModel() {
    var self = this;
    self.handleOpen = $("#buttonOpener").click(function() {
      $("#modalDialog1").ojDialog("open"); });
    self.handleOKClose = $("#okButton").click(function() {
      $("#modalDialog1").ojDialog("close"); });
  }
  $(function() {
    ko.applyBindings(new dialogModel(),
      document.getElementById('dialogWrapper'));
  });
});
```

The output should be displayed in the page:

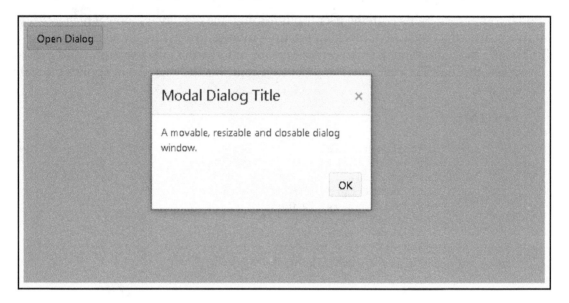

We can also have additional features such as progress bars, headers/footers, and animations associated with the dialog component.

Navigation lists

Application navigation is an important user experience concern in web application design. Oracle JET provides diverse navigation components for us to choose from and design our application as per the business context and choice:

- **HTML:**

```
<div id="navlistdemo">
  <div class="oj-flex oj-flex-items-pad">
    <div class="oj-flex-item">
      <label id="navigationLevellabelid">Navigation Level</label>
      <div id="navigationLevelRadioId"
       aria-labelledby="navigationLevellabelid"
       data-bind="ojComponent: {
         component: 'ojRadioset',
         value: navigationLevel}" >
        <span class="oj-choice-item">
          <input id="application" type="radio"
            name="navigationLevel" value="application">
```

```
          <label for="application">Application</label>
        </span>
        <span class="oj-choice-item">
          <input id="page" type="radio" name="navigationLevel"
           value="page">
          <label for="page">Page</label>
        </span>
      </div>
    </div>
    <div class="oj-flex-item">
      <label id="condenseLabel" for="condense">Condense</label>
      <input id="condense" data-bind="ojComponent: {
       component: 'ojSwitch', value: isChecked}" />
    </div>
    <div class="oj-flex-item">
      <label id="contrastBgLabel"
       for="contrastBgSwitch">Contrast Background</label>
      <input id="contrastBgSwitch" data-bind="ojComponent: {
       component: 'ojSwitch', value: isContrastBackground}" />
    </div>
  </div>
  <p>
    <h4>With Only Text </h4>
    <div class="navlistcontainer">
      <div aria-label="Choose a navigation item"
       data-bind="ojComponent:{
         component: 'ojNavigationList',
         drillMode: 'none',
         selection: 'home5',
         navigationLevel: navigationLevel,
         edge: 'top'}" >
        <ul >
          <li id="home5">
            <a href="#">Home</a>
          </li>
          <li id="gettingstarted5">
            <a href="#">Getting Started</a>
          </li>
          <li id="cookbook5">
            <a href="#">Cookbook</a>
          </li>
          <li id="stylelab5" class="oj-disabled">
            <a href="#">Style Lab</a>
          </li>
          <li id="library5" >
            <a href="#" >Library</a>
          </li>
        </ul>
```

```
          </div>
     </div>
     <h4>With Text and Icons</h4>
        <div class="navlistcontainer">
          <div aria-label="Choose a navigation item"
           data-bind="ojComponent:{
              component: 'ojNavigationList',
              drillMode: 'none',
              selection: 'home4',
              navigationLevel: navigationLevel,
              edge: 'top'}" >
          <ul>
            <li id="home4">
              <a href="#">
                <span class="oj-navigationlist-item-icon
                 demo-home-icon-24 demo-icon-font-24">
                </span>Home</a>
            </li>
            <li id="gettingstarted4">
              <a href="#">
                <span class="oj-navigationlist-item-icon
                 demo-education-icon-24 demo-icon-font-24">
                </span>Getting Started</a>
            </li>
            <li id="cookbook4">
              <a href="#">
                <span class="oj-navigationlist-item-icon
                  demo-catalog-icon-24 demo-icon-font-24">
                </span>Cookbook</a>
            </li>
            <li id="stylelab4" class="oj-disabled">
              <a href="#">
                <span class="oj-navigationlist-item-icon
                 demo-palette-icon-24 demo-icon-font-24">
                </span>Style Lab</a>
            </li>
            <li id="library4" >
              <a href="#" >
                <span class="oj-navigationlist-item-icon
                 demo-library-icon-24 demo-icon-font-24">
                </span>Library</a>
            </li>
          </ul>
        </div>
     </div>
     <h4> With only Icons</h4>
     <div class="navlistcontainer">
        <div aria-label="Choose a navigation item"
```

```
        data-bind="ojComponent:{
          component: 'ojNavigationList',
          drillMode: 'none',
          display:'icons',
          selection: 'home1',
          navigationLevel: navigationLevel,
          edge: 'top'}">
        <ul >
          <li id="home1">
            <a href="#">
              <span class="oj-navigationlist-item-icon
                demo-home-icon-24 demo-icon-font-24">
              </span>Home</a>
          </li>
          <li id="gettingstarted1">
            <a href="#">
              <span class="oj-navigationlist-item-icon
                demo-education-icon-24 demo-icon-font-24">
              </span>Getting Started</a>
          </li>
          <li id="cookbook1">
            <a href="#">
              <span class="oj-navigationlist-item-icon
                demo-catalog-icon-24 demo-icon-font-24">
              </span>Cookbook</a>
          </li>
          <li id="stylelab1" class="oj-disabled">
            <a href="#">
              <span class="oj-navigationlist-item-icon
                demo-palette-icon-24 demo-icon-font-24">
              </span>Style Lab</a>
          </li>
          <li id="library1" >
            <a href="#" >
              <span class="oj-navigationlist-item-icon
                demo-library-icon-24 demo-icon-font-24">
              </span>Library</a>
          </li>
        </ul>
      </div>
  </div>
<h4> With Stacked Label and Icon</h4>
<div class="navlistcontainer">
  <div aria-label="Choose a navigation item"
    data-bind="ojComponent:{
      component: 'ojNavigationList',
      drillMode: 'none',
      selection: 'home2',
```

```
                navigationLevel: navigationLevel,
                edge: 'top'}"
          class="oj-navigationlist-stack-icon-label">
          <ul>
            <li id="home2">
              <a href="#">
                <span class="oj-navigationlist-item-icon
                  demo-home-icon-24 demo-icon-font-24">
                </span>Home</a>
            </li>
            <li id="gettingstarted2">
              <a href="#">
                <span class="oj-navigationlist-item-icon
                  demo-education-icon-24 demo-icon-font-24">
                </span>Getting Started</a>
            </li>
            <li id="cookbook2">
              <a href="#">
                <span class="oj-navigationlist-item-icon
                  demo-catalog-icon-24 demo-icon-font-24">
                </span>Cookbook</a>
            </li>
            <li id="stylelab2" class="oj-disabled">
              <a href="#">
                <span class="oj-navigationlist-item-icon
                  demo-palette-icon-24 demo-icon-font-24">
                </span>Style Lab</a>
            </li>
            <li id="library2" >
              <a href="#" >
                <span class="oj-navigationlist-item-icon
                  demo-library-icon-24 demo-icon-font-24">
                </span>Library</a>
            </li>
          </ul>
        </div>
      </div>
    </div>
```

- **JavaScript:**

```javascript
require(['ojs/ojcore', 'knockout', 'jquery', 'ojs/ojknockout',
         'ojs/ojnavigationlist', 'ojs/ojswitch',
         'ojs/ojradioset' ],
function(oj, ko, $)
// this callback gets executed when all required
   modules are loaded
{
  $(function() {
    function ViewModel() {
      this.navigationLevel = ko.observable('page');
      this.isChecked = ko.observable();
      this.isChecked.subscribe(function(newValue) {
        var navlistInstances = $('#navlistdemo')
                                .find(':oj-navigationlist');
        if(newValue) {
          navlistInstances.addClass('oj-sm-condense');
        } else {
          navlistInstances.removeClass('oj-sm-condense');
        }
      });
      this.isContrastBackground = ko.observable(false);
      this.isContrastBackground.subscribe(function(newValue) {
        if(newValue) {
          $(".navlistcontainer").addClass("demo-panel-contrast1
                                   oj-contrast-marker");
        } else {
          $(".navlistcontainer").removeClass("demo-panel-contrast1
                                       oj-contrast-marker");
        }
      });
    }
    var vm = new ViewModel();
    ko.applyBindings(vm,
      document.getElementById('navlistdemo'));
  });
});
```

The output should be displayed in the page:

We can also have additional features such as condensed (having elements smaller and close to each other), contrast background (for more visual appeal), and responsive page navigation components.

Panels

Panel components let us display different sections in the page along with highlighting each panel in a different color palette. `oj-panel` helps us add a panel to the page, while `oj-panel-alt*` lets us get different colors for the panels:

- **HTML:**

```
<div id="panelPage">
  <div class="oj-flex">
    <div class="oj-panel oj-margin demo-panel-customizations">
      <i>default</i>
```

```
      </div>
      <div class="oj-panel oj-panel-alt1
       oj-margin demo-panel-customizations">Panel One
      </div>
      <div class="oj-panel oj-panel-alt2
       oj-margin demo-panel-customizations">Panel Two
      </div>
      <div class="oj-panel oj-panel-alt3
       oj-margin demo-panel-customizations">Panel Three
      </div>
      <div class="oj-panel oj-panel-alt4
       oj-margin demo-panel-customizations">Panel Four
      </div>
      <div class="oj-panel oj-panel-alt5
       oj-margin demo-panel-customizations">Panel Five
      </div>
    </div>
  </div>
```

- **CSS:**

```
.demo-panel-customizations {
  width:  100px;
  height: 100px;
}
```

The output should be displayed in the page:

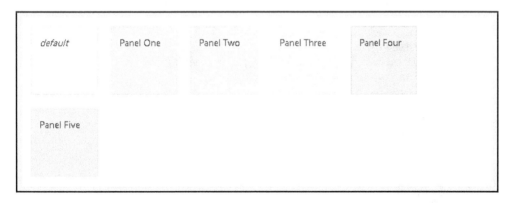

We can also have additional features such as affordances, shadows, and selected panels with this component.

Tabs

Tabs lets us populate a page with heavy content which can be split into groups and populated in each of the tabs. Previous versions of web applications used to have heavy tab components; however, Oracle JET has given us a simplified web version of the tab feature with ojTabs. The following example demonstrates the usage of tabs:

- **HTML:**

```html
<div id="tabs-container">
  <div id="tabs" data-bind="ojComponent:
   {component: 'ojTabs', disabledTabs: [3]}">
   <!-- tab bar -->
   <ul>
     <li><span>Tab One</span></li>
     <li><span>Tab Two</span></li>
     <li><span>Tab Three</span></li>
     <li><span>Disabled Tab</span></li>
   </ul>
   <!-- tab contents -->
   <div id="tabs-1">
     <p>Tab One Content</p>
   </div>
   <div id="tabs-2">
     <p>Tab Two Content</p>
   </div>
   <div id="tabs-3">
     <p>Tab Three Content</p>
   </div>
   <div id="tabs-4">
     <p>Disabled Tab Content</p>
   </div>
  </div>
</div>
```

- **JavaScript:**

```javascript
require(['ojs/ojcore', 'knockout', 'jquery', 'ojs/ojknockout',
         'ojs/ojtabs',  'ojs/ojconveyorbelt'],
function(oj, ko, $)
{
  $(function()
  {
```

```
      ko.applyBindings(null,
            document.getElementById('tabs-container'))
   });
});
```

The output should be displayed in the page:

We can also have additional features such as sortable, button-based, and vertical tabs, along with lazy content render features in the tab component.

Summary

In this chapter, we learned the advanced Oracle JET components and ways to use these visualization, layout, and navigation components. We also learned about different visualization components offered by the Oracle JET framework with examples. We finished this chapter with an understanding of how layouts and navigation components improve the user experience of dynamic web applications, and populate hierarchical data for the applications.

In the next chapter, we will learn about advanced Oracle JET framework topics such as validations, internationalization and localization, and application theming with Oracle JET in detail.

7
Framework

The strength of a framework lies not only in its rich form components, but also in its ability to address common application concerns seamlessly by providing additional tools and components that make the framework rich in features. Modern web applications are driven by responsive Spring page application architecture with routing frameworks in an efficient and responsive design. Oracle JET provides such productive features through its reusable components and support for common application requirements, which will be reviewed in this chapter.

In this chapter, we will cover:

- Application routing
- Validations and conversions
- Responsiveness
- Performance
- Internationalization and localization
- Accessibility
- Application theming

Application routing

Oracle JET provides a **Single-Page Application (SPA)** design for our application through the `ojModule` binding and `oj.Router` routing architecture. The way they work is through a content replacement technique by `ojModule` from `Knockout.js` with the content routing provided by `oj.Router`. The following diagram represents the difference between the traditional and Single-Page Application life cycle:

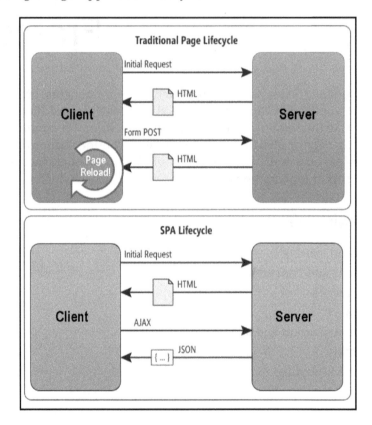

In a traditional page life cycle, each page gets loaded from the server to the client on request, and the page gets reloaded with the next page when the user tries to navigate through the application. In Single-Page Applications, the client loads the first page on initial request and when the user tries to navigate to the next page, an **AJAX** request is made to the **Server** to dynamically load the content and replace the view components with the desired elements, instead of a complete page reload.

The following is the basic routing example using the Oracle JET module and routing elements:

- **HTML:**

```html
<div id="sampleDemo" style="" class="demo-padding
demo-container">
  <div id="componentDemoContent" style="width: 1px;
  min-width: 100%;">
    <div id="routing-container">
      <oj-toolbar id='buttons-container'>
        <oj-buttonset-one class="oj-buttonset-width-auto"
        value="{{router.stateId}}" focus-management="none">
          <!-- ko foreach: router.states -->
            <oj-option value="[[id]]">
              <span data-bind="text: label"></span>
            </oj-option>
          <!-- /ko -->
        </oj-buttonset-one>
      </oj-toolbar>
      <hr/>
      <div id="pageContent" class="oj-panel oj-panel-alt2"
      style="width: 200px">
        <h3 data-bind="text: router.currentValue"></h3>
      </div>
    </div>
  </div>
</div>
```

- **JavaScript:**

```javascript
require(['ojs/ojcore', 'knockout', 'jquery', 'ojs/ojknockout',
'ojs/ojtoolbar', 'ojs/ojbutton', 'ojs/ojrouter'],
function(oj, ko, $)
{
  var base = document.getElementsByTagName('base')
  [0].getAttribute('href');
  oj.Router.defaults['baseUrl'] = base;
  // Retrieve the router static instance and
  // configure the states
  var router = oj.Router.rootInstance;
  router.configure(
  {
    'homepage': { label: 'Home', value: 'This is the Home Page.',
    isDefault: true },
    'page1': { label: 'Page 1', value: 'This is the Page 1.' },
    'page2': { label: 'Page 2', value: 'This is the Page 2.' },
    'page3': { label: 'Page 3', value: 'This is the Page 3.' }
```

```
        });
        var viewModel =
        {
           router: router
        };
        $(function()
        {
           ko.applyBindings(viewModel,
           document.getElementById('routing-container'));
           oj.Router.sync();
        });
     });
```

The output should be displayed on the page as follows:

You can click on either of the pages using the navigation provided on top to check the content for that page, as follows:

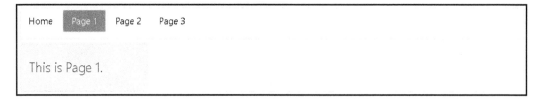

Oracle JET supports nested routers, navigation, arbitrary storage, and wizards with routing components.

Validations and conversions

Oracle JET provides multiple validation and conversion components to help us manage diverse application and component validations, and date value conversions. In the following section, let's review both validations and conversions provided by the framework.

Validations

It is important to validate the user input before submitting it for server interaction and sending data over the secure network. These validations include component-based data validation and application level validation; both are handled seamlessly by the framework components.

Component validations

Component validations include field validations for input components. They are applied to each field explicitly based on the field data type and expected content for that field, starting from mandatory field validation to the field length validation to complex field expression validations. The following is an example of component validation using validators and required validators, which trigger validations `on-value-changed`:

- **HTML**:

```
<div id="sampleDemo" style=""
class="demo-padding demo-container">
  <div id="componentDemoContent" style="width: 1px;
  min-width: 100%;">
    <div id="validation-usecase"
    class="oj-form oj-md-odd-cols-4 oj-md-labels-inline
    oj-sm-odd-cols-12">
      <div class="oj-flex">
        <div class="oj-flex-item">
          <oj-label for="username" show-required>User Name
          </oj-label>
        </div>
        <div class="oj-flex-item">
          //input text component with validation attributes
          <oj-input-text id="username" autocomplete="off"
           required validators="[[validators]]"
           on-value-changed="[[valueChangedListener]]"
           name="username" value="{{userName}}"
           placeholder="Enter at least 3 alphanumeric characters">
```

```
            </oj-input-text>
            <span id="status" title="Initial isValid Flag"
             role="img" class="oj-fwk-icon-status-error oj-fwk-icon"
             data-bind="style: {
                display: userNameIsNotValid() ?
                'inline-block': 'none'}">
            </span>
        </div>
    </div>
    <div class="oj-flex">
        <div class="oj-flex-item">
            <oj-label for="password" show-required>Password
            </oj-label>
        </div>
        <div class="oj-flex-item">
        // password component with vaidation attribute
        <oj-input-password id="password"
         autocomplete="off" required
         validators="[[validators2]]"
         name="password"
         value="{{password}}"
         on-value-changed="[[valueChangedListener]]"
         help.instruction="Enter at least 6 characters
         including a number, one uppercase and
         lowercase letter">
        </oj-input-password>
        <span id="pwdstatus" title="Deferred Error"
         role="img"
         class="oj-fwk-icon-status-error oj-fwk-icon"
         data-bind="style: {display: passwordIsNotValid() ?
         'inline-block': 'none'}">
        </span>
    </div>
    </div>
    <div class="oj-flex">
      <div class="oj-flex-item"></div>
        <div class="oj-flex-item">
          <oj-button id="showMsgsBtn"
           data-bind="click: showMessages">Submit</oj-button>
        </div>
      </div>
    </div>
  </div>
</div>
```

- **JavaScript:**

```
require(['ojL10n!nls/MessageBundle', 'ojs/ojcore',
  'knockout', 'jquery', 'ojs/ojknockout','ojs/ojinputtext',
  'ojs/ojbutton', 'ojs/ojlabel'],
  function (bundle, oj, ko, $)
  // this callback gets executed when all required
  // modules for validation are loaded
  {
    function DemoViewModel()
    {
      var self = this;
      self.tracker = ko.observable();
      // for username field
      self.userName = ko.observable();
      self.userNameIsNotValid = ko.observable(false);
      // for password field
      self.password = ko.observable();
      self.passwordIsNotValid = ko.observable(false);
      self.validators = ko.computed(function()
      {
        return [{
          type: 'regExp',
          options: {
            pattern: '[a-zA-Z0-9]{3,}',
            messageDetail: 'You must enter at least 3
          letters or numbers'}
        }];
      });
      self.validators2 = ko.computed(function()
      {
        return [{
          type: 'regExp',
          options : {
          pattern: '(?=.*\\d)(?=.*[a-z])(?=.*[A-Z]).{6,}',
          label: 'Password',
          messageSummary : '\'{label}\' too Weak',
          messageDetail:
          'You must enter a password that meets
          our minimum security requirements.'}}];
      });
      self.valueChangedListener = function(event)
      {
        var id = event.currentTarget.id;
        if (id === "username")
        {
          self.userNameIsNotValid(false);
        }
```

```
              else
              {
                self.passwordIsNotValid(false);
              }
           };
           // Calls showMessages method on each component
           self.showMessages = function ()
           {
             var element1 = document.getElementById("username");
             var element2 = document.getElementById("password");
             element1.showMessages();
             element2.showMessages();
             self.userNameIsNotValid(
             !(element1.validate()));
             self.passwordIsNotValid(
             !(element2.validate()));
           }
        };
        $(
           function()
           {
             $("#showMsgsBtn").on('click', function () {
               document.getElementById('username').showMessages();
               document.getElementById('password').showMessages();
             });
             ko.applyBindings(new DemoViewModel(),
             document.getElementById('validation-usecase'));
           }
        );
     });
```

The output should be displayed on the page as follows:

* User Name	*Enter at least 3 alphanumeric characters*
* Password	
	Submit

Enter just two characters in the **User Name** and **Password** fields and move the field focus away from them. Click on the **Submit** button to see the validations of the fields highlighted:

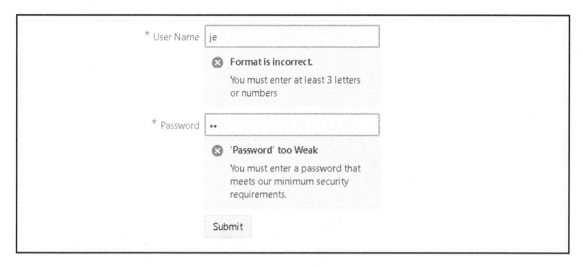

The moment you enter the expected field values as per the validation advised in the form, you can see the page allowing you to submit, as shown in the following screenshot:

The component validations of the `oj` validation framework do support value option changes, refreshing the component value on change, trigger method validation, and invoking multiple validator options.

Application level validations

Application level validations include the field validations to be applied based on certain preconditions, such as the selection of another component or a value-driven choice. Complex application validations include validation on more than one field value.

In the following example, you can observe that based on the `Validate By` field selection, the application level validation applies to either the email or phone number fields.

- **HTML:**

```
<div id="sampleDemo" style=""
class="demo-padding demo-container">
  <div id="componentDemoContent" style="width: 1px;
  min-width: 100%;">
    <div id="componentDemo">
      <div id="crossfield-example"
      class="oj-form oj-md-odd-cols-4 oj-md-labels-inline
      oj-sm-odd-cols-12">
      <hr>
        <h1>User Registration</h1>
        <hr>
          <div class="oj-flex">
            <div class="oj-flex-item">
            <oj-label id="brblabel">Validate By</oj-label>
            </div>
            <div class="oj-flex-item">
              <oj-radioset id="radioSetId"
              labelled-by="brblabel"
              value='{{contactPref}}'>
                <oj-option id="opt1" value="email">Email
                </oj-option>
                <oj-option id="opt2" value="phone">Phone
                </oj-option>
              </oj-radioset>
            </div>
          </div>
          <div class="oj-flex">
            <div class="oj-flex-item">
              <oj-label for="emailId">Email Address
              </oj-label>
            </div>
            <div class="oj-flex-item">
              <oj-input-text id="emailId"
              type="email" name="emailId"
              placeholder="john_doe@example.com"
              value="{{emailAddress}}"
              messages-custom="{{emailAddressMessages}}"
              disabled="[[contactPref() !== 'email']]">
              </oj-input-text>
            </div>
          </div>
          <div class="oj-flex">
            <div class="oj-flex-item">
```

```
                <oj-label for="telNum">Phone Number
                </oj-label>
              </div>
              <div class="oj-flex-item">
                <oj-input-text id="telNum" name="telNum"
                help.instruction="US phone number"
                placeholder="ten digit phone number"
                value="{{phoneNumber}}"
                messages-custom="{{phoneNumberMessages}}"
                disabled="[[contactPref() !== 'phone']]"
                validators="[[validators]]"></oj-input-text>
              </div>
            </div>
            <hr>
            <div class="oj-flex">
              <div class="oj-flex-item">
                <oj-button id="create"
                disabled="[[shouldDisableCreate]]"
                on-click="[[createNewMember]]" >Submit
                </oj-button>
              </div>
            </div>
          </div>
        </div>
      </div>
    </div>
```

- **JavaScript**:

```javascript
require(['ojL10n!nls/MessageBundle', 'ojs/ojcore',
'knockout', 'jquery', 'ojs/ojradioset', 'ojs/ojinputtext',
'ojs/ojbutton', 'ojs/ojlabel'],
function (bundle, oj, ko, $)
{
  function CrossFieldValidator(options)
  {
    this._options = options;
  }
  ;
  CrossFieldValidator.prototype.validate =
  function (valueOnDependent)
  {
    var summary, detail, params,
    validatorOptions = this._options;
    if (validatorOptions)
    {
      var baseObs = validatorOptions['base'];
      if (baseObs)
```

```
    {
      var baseValue = ko.utils.unwrapObservable(baseObs);
      var triggerValue = validatorOptions['baseTriggerValue'];
      if ((triggerValue && baseValue &&
      triggerValue === baseValue) && !valueOnDependent)
      {
        params = {'label': validatorOptions['label']};
        summary = oj.Translations.applyParameters(
        bundle['app']
        ['validator-crossField']['summary'], params);
        detail = oj.Translations.applyParameters(
        bundle['app']
        ['validator-crossField']['detail'], params);
        throw new oj.ValidatorError(summary, detail);
      }
    }
  }
  return true;
};
function MemberViewModel()
{
  var self = this;
  // for invalidComponentTracker attribute
  self.tracker = ko.observable();
  var formElements = [document.getElementById("emailId"),
                      document.getElementById("telNum")];
  var ContactPref = {'EMAIL': 'email', 'PHONE': 'phone'};
  self.contactPref = ko.observable(ContactPref['EMAIL']);
  self.validators = ko.computed(function()
  {
    return [{type: 'regExp', options : {
      pattern: '\\d{10}',
      hint: 'enter a ten digit phone number including \n\
      area code with no spaces or special characters',
      messageSummary: 'Value \'{value}\' Invalid',
      messageDetail: 'You must enter a 10 digit phone \n\
      number starting with area code.'}}];
  });
  // emailAddress must be set when contact pref is 'email'
  self.emailAddrCRValidator = new CrossFieldValidator({
  base: self.contactPref,
  baseTriggerValue: ContactPref['EMAIL'],
  label: 'Email Address'});
  self.emailAddress = ko.observable();
  self.emailAddressMessages = ko.observableArray([]);
  // phoneNumber must have a value when
  // the contactPref is 'phone'
  self.phoneNumCRValidator = new CrossFieldValidator({
```

```
      base: self.contactPref,
      baseTriggerValue: ContactPref['PHONE'],
      label: 'Phone Number'});
  self.phoneNumber = ko.observable();
  self.phoneNumberMessages = ko.observableArray([]);
  var clearMessagesOnDependentsOfContactPref =
  function (newValue) {
  if (newValue === ContactPref['EMAIL'] ||
  newValue === ContactPref['PHONE'])
  {
    self.phoneNumberMessages([]);
    self.emailAddressMessages([]);
  }
};
self.contactPref.subscribe
(clearMessagesOnDependentsOfContactPref);
self.shouldDisableCreate = ko.observable(false);
self.createNewMember = function (event)
{
  // Step 1
  self._showComponentValidationErrors()
  .then(function(values) {
    for (var j=0; j < values.length; j++)
    {
      if (values[j] === "invalid") {
        return;
      }
    }
    // Step 2
    if (!self._runAppLevelValidation())
      return;
    });
  };
  self._showComponentValidationErrors = function ()
  {
    var length = formElements.length;
    var promises = [];
    for (var i=0; i< length; i++)
    {
      // don't push disabled components to be validated.
      if (!formElements[i].disabled)
      // validate will show messages, if any
      promises.push(formElements[i].validate());
    }
    return Promise.all(promises);
  };
  self._runAppLevelValidation = function ()
  {
```

```
             var valid = true;
             valid = (this._validateObservable(this.emailAddress,
             this.emailAddrCRValidator,
             this.emailAddressMessages) &&
             this._validateObservable(this.phoneNumber,
             this.phoneNumCRValidator,
             this.phoneNumberMessages));
             if (!valid)
             {
               return false;
             }
             return true;
          };
          self._validateObservable = function
          (obs, validator, messages)
          {
             var message, valid = true, msgs = [];
             try
             {
               // clear all messages before validating property
               messages([]);
               validator.validate(ko.utils.unwrapObservable(obs));
             } catch (e)
             {
               if (e instanceof oj.ValidatorError)
               {
               message = e.getMessage();
               } else
               {
                 var summary =
                 e.message ? e.message :
                 bundle['app']['validation-failed'];
                 message = {summary:summary, detail:"",
                 severity: oj.Message.SEVERITY_LEVEL.ERROR};
               }
               valid = false;
               msgs.push(message);
               messages(msgs);
             }
             return valid;
          };
      } ;
      $(
         function ()
         {
           ko.applyBindings(new MemberViewModel(),
           document.getElementById('crossfield-example'));
         });
```

```
});
```

The output should be displayed on the page as follows:

If you directly submit the form, you can see that the field validation is applied only on the **Email** field, as follows:

However, by changing the `Validate By` selection to **Phone** and submitting the form again, you can observe that the validation is triggered for the **Phone Number** instead, as shown in the following screenshot:

User Registration

Validate By ○ Email
● Phone

Email Address *john_doe@example.com*

Phone Number | *ten digit phone number* |

❌ **Phone Number Required**
You must enter a value for field
Phone Number

Submit

By entering the value of either the email or phone number based on the `Validate By` field selection, you can pass through the validation and submit the form.

Along with the component and user-level validations, you can make use of either of the following versatile validators: date time range validator, date restriction validator, length validator, number range validator, regexp validator, required validator, and custom validator.

Converters

Converters help by transforming the value obtained to the presentable form, which is especially useful when dealing with currency, date, and number fields. In the following example, we will review the date time converter provided by the framework:

- **HTML:**

```
<div id="sampleDemo" style=""
class="demo-padding demo-container">
  <div id="componentDemoContent" style="width: 1px;
```

```
min-width: 100%;">
  <div id="datetime-converter-example">
    <h3 class="oj-header-border">Date and Time</h3>
    <p>Converts between locale specific date and
    time string and Date value. </p>
    <div class="oj-form oj-md-odd-cols-4 oj-md-labels-inline">
      <div class="oj-flex">
        <div class="oj-flex-item">
          <oj-label for="datetime2">input datetime</oj-label>
        </div>
        <div class="oj-flex-item">
          //date time component with converter attribute
          <oj-input-date-time id="datetime2"
          value="{{datetime}}" name="datetime2"
          help.instruction="enter a date in your
          preferred format and we will attempt
          to figure it out"
          converter= '{
            "type":"datetime",
            "options": {"formatType": "datetime",
            "dateFormat": "short"}}'>
          </oj-input-date-time>
        </div>
      </div>
      <div class="oj-flex">
        <div class="oj-flex-item">
          <oj-label for="text20">input text</oj-label>
        </div>
        <div class="oj-flex-item">
          //input text component with datetime converter
          <oj-input-text id="text20"
          value="{{datetime}}" name="text20"
          help.instruction="enter a date in your
          preferred format and we will attempt to
          figure it out"
          converter= '{
            "type":"datetime",
            "options": {"formatType": "datetime",
            "dateFormat": "short",
            "timeFormat": "short"}}'>
          </oj-input-text>
        </div>
      </div>
    </div>
  </div>
</div>
```

- **JavaScript**:

```
require(['ojs/ojcore', 'knockout', 'jquery',
'ojs/ojknockout', 'ojs/ojdatetimepicker', 'ojs/ojlabel'],
function(oj, ko, $)
{
  function MemberViewModel()
  {
    var self = this;
    self.date = ko.observable();
    self.datetime = ko.observable();
    self.time = ko.observable();
  };
  $(
    function()
    {
      ko.applyBindings(new MemberViewModel(),
      document.getElementById('datetime-converter-example'));
    }
  );
});
```

The output should be displayed on the page, and you can select any date and time as shown in the following screenshot:

You can change the value of the datetime field or simple text field to reflect the changes, as long as you enter the value in the correct format.

Similarly, the framework provides the number converter, converter factory, and custom converters to support diverse requirements.

Responsiveness

Responsive web design is provided by the Oracle JET framework for the web pages with the help of fluid grids, scalable images, and media queries. The framework has an exhaustive 12-column grid system and form layouts with styles for different sized screen devices. Grid and Media queries help the pages to render as per the screen resolution. Let us quickly review an example form layout and how it varies between a desktop and a mobile screen, as follows:

- **HTML:**

```
<div id="sampleDemo" style="" class="demo-padding
 demo-container">
  <div id="componentDemoContent" style="width: 1px;
  min-width: 100%;">
    <div id="form-container">
      <p>Demo width in
        <span class="demo-screen-range"></span>
      screen range.</p>
      <div class="oj-form-layout">
      // input form components with style classes for layout
        <div class="oj-form oj-sm-odd-cols-12
        oj-lg-odd-cols-4 oj-lg-labels-inline
        oj-form-cols oj-form-cols-max2" >
          <div class="oj-flex">
            <div class="oj-flex-item">
              <oj-label show-required for="inputcontrol">input 1
              </oj-label>
            </div>
            <div class="oj-flex-item">
              <oj-input-text id="inputcontrol" required
               value="text">
              </oj-input-text>
            </div>
          </div>
          <div class="oj-flex">
            <div class="oj-flex-item">
              <oj-label for="textareacontrol">textarea
              </oj-label>
            </div>
            <div class="oj-flex-item">
              <oj-text-area id="textareacontrol"
              value='text' rows="6">
              </oj-text-area>
            </div>
          </div>
```

```
          <div class="oj-flex">
            <div class="oj-flex-item">
              <oj-label for="inputcontrol2">input 2
              </oj-label>
            </div>
            <div class="oj-flex-item">
              <oj-input-text id="inputcontrol2" value="text">
              </oj-input-text>
            </div>
          </div>

        <div class="oj-flex">
          <div class="oj-flex-item">
            <oj-label for="inputcontrol3">input 3 longer label
            </oj-label>
          </div>
          <div class="oj-flex-item">
            <oj-input-text id="inputcontrol3" value="text">
            </oj-input-text>
          </div>
        </div>

        <div class="oj-flex">
          <div class="oj-flex-item">
            <oj-label for="inputcontrol4">input 4</oj-label>
          </div>
          <div class="oj-flex-item">
            <oj-input-text id="inputcontrol4" value="text">
            </oj-input-text>
          </div>
        </div>

        <div class="oj-flex">
          <div class="oj-flex-item">
            <oj-label for="inputcontrol5">input 5</oj-label>
          </div>
          <div class="oj-flex-item">
            <oj-input-text id="inputcontrol5" value="text">
            </oj-input-text>
          </div>
        </div>

        <div class="oj-flex">
          <div class="oj-flex-item">
            <oj-label for="inputcontrol6">input 6</oj-label>
          </div>
          <div class="oj-flex-item">
            <oj-input-text id="inputcontrol6" value="text">
```

```
          </oj-input-text>
        </div>
      </div>
    </div>
  </div>
 </div>
</div>
```

- **JavaScript:**

```
require(['ojs/ojcore', 'knockout', 'jquery',
        'ojs/ojlabel', 'ojs/ojknockout', 'ojs/ojinputtext'],
function(oj, ko, $)
{
  $(function()
  {
    ko.applyBindings(null,
          document.getElementById('form-container'));
  });
});
```

By running this page on a desktop screen you can see the following:

Demo width in **lg** screen range.

* input 1	text		input 2	text
textarea	text		input 3 longer label	text
			input 4	text
			input 5	text
			input 6	text

If you run the same application in a mobile web browser, you will see the following:

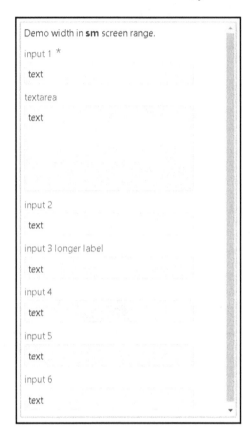

You can clearly observe the differences in form layout, adjusted according to the screen size.

Media queries

CSS-based @media queries help in bringing the required layout at rule, media type, and expression-based value advise. The following code shows the syntax of media query usage in CSS:

```
<style>
  @media media_types (expression){
    /* media-specific rules */
  }
</style>
```

The following table represents different screen pixel ranges and corresponding devices:

Size	Pixel Range	Device
Small	0 – 767	Mobile Phone
Medium	768 – 1023	Tablet (portrait)
Large	1024 – 1279	Desktop, Tablet (landscape)
Extra Large	1280 – 1440	Desktop (large)

Oracle JET framework offers a set of grid style classes with which we can obtain the desired layout on the page. Some of the important grid style classes are presented in the following table:

Grid Style Class	Purpose
oj-row	Place on a row.
oj-col	Place on each column.
oj-cols-nopad	Place on a row or its parent to remove column padding. By default, columns have padding.
oj-size-numberofcolumns	Set the column width.
oj-size-offset-numberofoffsetcolumns	Move columns over. Offset classes are not generated for small screens as there usually is not enough screen real estate to require these classes on small screens.
oj-size-center	Center columns.
oj-size-odd-cols-numberofcolumns	Use this in a 2-column layout. Instead of putting sizing classes on every column, you can put a single class on the row parent
oj-size-even-cols-numberofcolumns	Use in a 4-column layout. In this layout, you must use both the odd-cols class to control the width of odd numbered columns and the even-cols class to control the width of the even columns.

Performance

Application performance plays a key role in client user experience and can be optimized by following certain standards and mechanisms, as follows:

1. Cache optimization.
2. Reducing the client-server calls (network traffic).
3. Reducing the page size with caching.
4. Reducing the request content.
5. Optimizing the page layout.
6. Lightweight mobile design.

Similarly, Oracle JET offers certain optimization recommendations separately for JavaScript and CSS.

JavaScript optimization techniques

The following are the optimization techniques for best JavaScript usage advised by Oracle JET:

1. Minimize the JavaScript to the content required by a specific page.
2. Use a minified version of JavaScript libraries.
3. Reduce the content size to populate JavaScript.
4. Lazy loading on initial request.
5. Cache header usage.
6. Payload compression.

CSS optimization techniques

The following are the optimization techniques for best CSS usage advised by Oracle JET:

1. Minimize the CSS to the content required by a specific page.
2. Use a minified version of CSS.
3. Reduce the content size to populate the page's CSS.

In addition to the preceding JavaScript and CSS optimization techniques, Oracle JET offers certain framework component optimization techniques as follows.

Oracle JET component optimization techniques

1. Use the appropriate Oracle JET component for content rendering.
2. Follow the framework standards.
3. Use only a limited number of components per page.
4. Limit the number of web service requests per page.

Internationalization and localization

Global application support can be provided by web applications by giving proper internationalization and globalization support.

The following diagram shows a list of languages supported by Oracle JET through Oracle **National Language Support** (**NLS**):

Language	Language Tag	Language	Language Tag
Arabic	ar	Korean	ko
Brazilian Portuguese	pt	Norwegian	no
Canadian French	fr-CA	Polish	pl
Czech	cs	Portuguese	pt-PT
Danish	da	Romania	ro
Dutch	nl	Russian	ru
Finnish	fi	Simplified Chinese	zh-Hans
French	fr	Slovak	sk
German	de	Spanish	es
Greek	el	Swedish	sv
Hebrew	he	Thai	th
Hungarian	hu	Traditional Chinese	zh-Hant
Italian	it	Turkish	tr
Japanese	ja		

Additionally, Oracle JET offers support for over 160 locales by using the **Common Locale Data Repository** (**CLDR**), saved in the same way as locale bundles. The locale-specific information can be advised in the application in either:

- Requiring JS configuration
- Using the `lang` attribute in an HTML page
- Using the `navigator.language` or `navigator.userLanguage` browser properties

Oracle JET framework also lets us define translation bundles for labels on the page, to populate different language-specific labels on the page dynamically.

The sample program for the translation bundle is as follows:

```
define({
  "root": {
    "label": "Select an application",
    "menu1": "Payroll",
    "menu2": "Business Processing",
    "menu3": "Administration"
  },
  "fr": true,
  "cs": true
});
```

Accessibility

Accessibility features make the application accessible by those with disabilities, as well. Designing applications with the following features makes them accessible:

1. Making the application accessible without a mouse and only with a keyboard.
2. Providing assistance with content magnifiers and text readers.
3. Minimizing the usage of animations and timer features.

To build an application with such abilities, Oracle JET came up with following features:

1. **Navigation with touch and keyboard**: By following the **WAI-ARIA** (**Web Accessibility Initiative-Accessible Rich Internet Applications**) standards, Oracle JET provides the ability to access its components with touch and keyboard-based navigation. We can create landmarks on the page with these standards, including regions for the banner, navigation, main, and complementary landmarks using the attribute role.

2. **Magnifier**: Oracle JET provides the support for magnifying the page content with the help of browser zoom features.

3. **Text readers**: Oracle JET lets the content in WAI-ARIA standard and has support for screen text readers.

4. **Components**: Oracle JET components are designed for a suitable purpose and each of them have associated names and roles to be recognized.

5. **High color contrast**: With the trendy Alta UI theme, Oracle JET framework supports 4.5:1 luminous contrast as well. The `oj-hicontrast` class is available in Oracle JET framework to construct high contrast modes for our application. The framework also recommends using high contrast images with no background to build the application in high contrast mode.

6. **Hide screen readers content**: This feature is useful when you want to populate some content which is hidden for a sighted user. The `oj-helper-hiddenaccessible` class is provided by the Oracle JET framework and creates the content to be available for the screen readers but not visible to the sighted user.

Application theming

Oracle JET as a framework uses Oracle Alta UI for its application user experience design. While we can choose the default theme provided by the framework, we can also customize the application theme as per the business context. The level of customization the framework allows is to include or exclude the style components in the application.

1. The Alta UI theme offers the following style components for the application: `oj-alta.css`, `oj-alta-min.css`, `oj-alta-notag.css`, and `oj-alta-notag-min.css`.

2. It is recommended you use HTML5 page standards with the DOCTYPE as follows: `<!DOCTYPE html>`.

3. Oracle JET also contains a set of SCSS tools that easily read the style contents and apply them to the application.

Customized application theming

There are different ways to customize the application theme in Oracle JET. Let us review the Oracle JET Marker styles before explaining the customizing scenarios.

The following are the set of Marker styles offered by the Oracle JET framework, which can be used instead of CSS3 or CSS4 pseudo classes:

Marker Style	Purpose	Description
`oj-hicontrast`	Accessibility	To configure high contrast mode, can be applied on body tag
`oj-component`	Component	The root DOM element of a widget
`oj-visited`	Link	To apply when the user visits the element

`oj-disabled`
`oj-enabled`
`oj-read-only`
`oj-invalid`
`oj-warning`
`oj-required`
`oj-indeterminate`
	Input	Applied on input components to attribute the behavior

`oj-active`
`oj-selected`
`oj-hover`
`oj-focus`
`oj-focus-only`
`oj-default`
	User Action	Capture the user action and apply corresponding styles

`oj-expanded` `oj-collapsed`	Collapsible	To be associated with the elements having the expand/collapse feature

`oj-right`
`oj-center`
`oj-left`
`oj-start`
`oj-end`
	Alignment	Help in component alignments horizontally

`oj-top`
`oj-middle`
`oj-bottom`
	Alignment	Help in component alignments vertically

`oj-draggable`
`oj-drag`
`oj-drop`
`Xoj-valid-drop`
`oj-invalid-drop`
	Drag and Drop	To be used with the drag and drop components

Customizing the application theme using Sass

Oracle JET application themes can be customized using **Sass (Syntactically Awesome Style Sheets)**. The following are the steps involved in customizing the application theme using Sass:

1. Install both Sass and Ruby software on the system from their home page: `http://sass-lang.com/install`.

2. The following command needs to be executed to install Sass:

   ```
   gem install sass
   ```

3. To define the custom style configuration, create the `scss` file with the `filename.scss` naming standard or copy the theme's setting file from `_oj.alta.settings.scss`.

4. Add the custom configurations in the newly created file.

5. You can add the custom styling components for each of the `oj` components, such as `_myCustomProgressBar.scss`, by overriding the actual `ojProgressbar` framework component.

6. Once each of the custom components are defined, you can create an aggregation of the SCSS files to replace the override files.

7. Oracle JET lets you control what components will be included in your actual application CSS as well.

Customizing the application theme using Theme Builder

Oracle JET framework offers a *Theme Builder* application to let us visually customize the configurations we want to have, component wise, in our application.

You can refer to the global examples of custom themes in Oracle JET at:
`http://www.oracle.com/webfolder/technetwork/jet/globalExamples-ThemeViewer.html`.

Theme Builder for Oracle JET is available online at:
`http://www.oracle.com/webfolder/technetwork/jet-320/public_samples/JET-Theme-Builder/public_html/index.html`.

You will see the set of components along with the theme options, as shown in the following screenshot:

Layout and navigation controls can be customized using the following perspective:

The form components view can be customized using the following perspective:

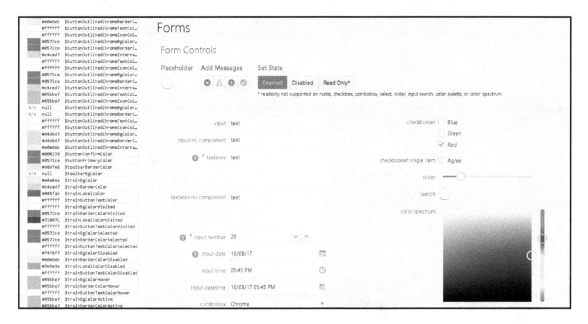

The data collection components view can be customized using the following perspective:

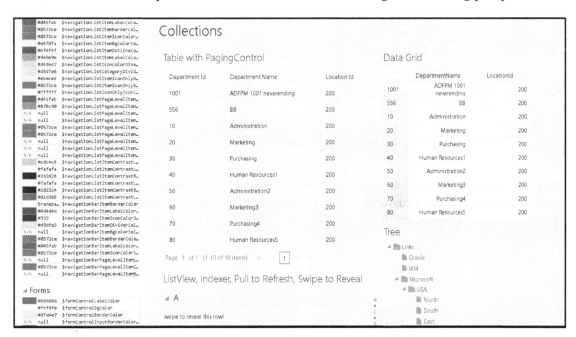

The data visualization components view can be customized using the following perspective:

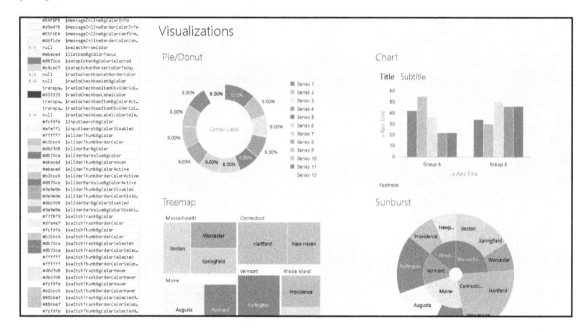

While there are an exhaustive set of customizations allowed, we have presented only the start of controls in the preceding screenshots. You can switch between the controls, layout and navigation, forms, collections, and visualizations.

 You can also see how the components look on different devices after customization. There is also a set of instructions designed for customization at:
http://www.oracle.com/webfolder/technetwork/jet-320/public_ samples/JET-Theme-Builder/public_html/index.html?root=library doc=docintroduction.

Overall, the framework offers a complete set of components for the standard and latest requirements, along with customizations that make the application more intuitive and accessible to diverse user groups across devices.

Summary

Throughout this chapter, we learnt about the advanced Oracle JET framework features including application routing and how to validate and convert the page content. We also learnt about responsiveness, improving performance, and internationalization and localization support from Oracle JET for applications. We finished this chapter by gaining an understanding of how Oracle JET applications are accessible to people with disabilities, and how to customize the application theme to best suit our business context.

In the next chapter, we will learn about hybrid mobile application development with the Oracle JET framework in detail.

8
Hybrid Mobile Application Development

Modern web development frameworks have numerous features, including the support for responsive web design and Single-Page Applications. The Oracle JET framework is one of the very few web frameworks that has the support for hybrid mobile application development. The framework chooses to use the standard designs and component patterns that best suit diverse mobile operating systems including iOS, Android, and Windows. Oracle JET mobile tools seamlessly integrate with other software packages to provide a rich development experience for hybrid mobile applications.

In this chapter, we will cover:

- Oracle JET mobile tools
- Hybrid mobile application development
- Packaging and publishing a mobile application

Oracle JET mobile tools

Mobile tools are the sets of software required to develop hybrid mobile applications. Oracle JET provides hybrid mobile application development support using Cordova. We need to install mobile tools specific to the operating system after confirming that we have the prerequisite software (installed in `Chapter 1`, *Getting Started with Oracle JET*), including npm, Node.js, Grunt, Bower, and Yeoman. In this section, let's review the important software for hybrid mobile application development with Oracle JET.

Cordova

While there are a number of mobile development frameworks, one of the popular open source frameworks is Apache Cordova, which supports the usage of standard web technologies such as HTML, CSS, and JavaScript to build applications supporting multiple platforms. This is achieved by delivering the applications in container wrapping, matching the target platforms with APIs that support native device features and content.

The following is the Apache Cordova application communication model that lets the application interact with the mobile operating system features using Cordova plugins:

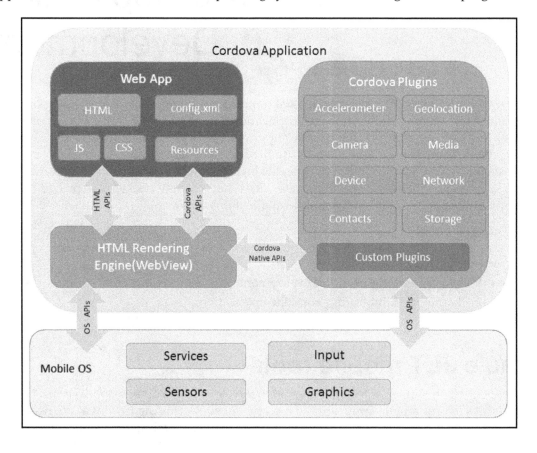

Using the following command, we can install the Cordova command-line tool; remember, the npm is a prerequisite to execute this command:

```
npm install -g cordova
```

Once Cordova is installed, we can create the application using the following command:

```
cordova create hybrid com.mobile.hybrid HybridProject
```

We can add the tools that support diverse mobile platforms, including iOS and Android, using the following commands:

```
cordova platform add ios
```

```
cordova platform add android
```

Once you develop the application components, you can build them using the following command:

```
cordova build
```

You can use the following command to build the components specific to the iOS platform:

```
cordova build ios
```

To test the application on diverse platforms from your desktop, you can use emulators. Emulators provide the environment, such as the target mobile platform, to let us test the application behavior on the target platform. For example, to emulate the Android platform we can use the following command:

```
cordova emulate android
```

Once the preceding command is executed, it launches the emulator launch window as shown in the following screenshot:

We can also run the application directly on a mobile by connecting it to the system and running the following command:

```
cordova run android
```

We can install the Android/iOS SDK to develop the components specific to the Android/iOS platform, as advised in their respective install guides:

Cordova Android Guide: `https://cordova.apache.org/docs/en/latest/guide/platforms/android/index.html`.

Cordova IOS Guide: `https://cordova.apache.org/docs/en/latest/guide/platforms/ios/index.html`.

Hybrid mobile application development

Once the mobile tools are installed as advised in the above steps, we can get started with hybrid mobile application development. Oracle JET provides the mobile tooling commands for creating, building, and running the hybrid mobile application on Android/iOS mobile devices. Based on the platform and application nature, we can create any of the following template-based applications:

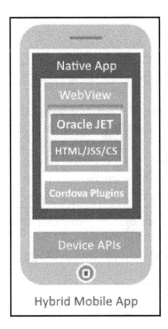

Oracle JET applications can be created using the following `yo oraclejet:hybrid` command, including the additional parameters. The complete syntax is advised, which is as follows:

```
yo oraclejet:hybrid [directory] [--appId=reverse-domain-style-identifier]
[--appName=application-display-title] [--template={template-name|template-
url}] [--platforms=android,ios]
```

Each parameter in the preceding syntax is important, as described in the following table:

Sr.No	Parameter	Description
1	directory	With `directory` on the filesystem, the application should get created. The application is created in the current working directory, if the directory is not specified.
2	appId	The application ID entered in reverse domain style, `com.mydomain`. It is equivalent to the package name on Android and bundle ID on iOS. If not specified, the `appId` defaults to `org.oraclejet.directory`, using the current directory or the directory you specified in the scaffolding command. For example, if you specified `app` for the directory, the default `appID` will be `org.oracle.jet.app`.
3	appName	Application name to be displayed on the device. You can include spaces in the title by using quotes, for example: `--appName="Mobile Application"`.
4	template	The template to be used for this application. Specify either of the following: template-name: Predefined template names, either blank, navBar, or navDrawer. Blank is the default template if this option is not specified. template-URL: URL for the ZIP file containing the name of the zipped application. For example, `http://application-path/app-name.zip`.
5	platforms	You can specify one or more platforms, comma separated, for example: `ios, android`. The command will prompt us for our choice of platform, if this option is not specified.

The following screenshot represents the application view created with a Blank template:

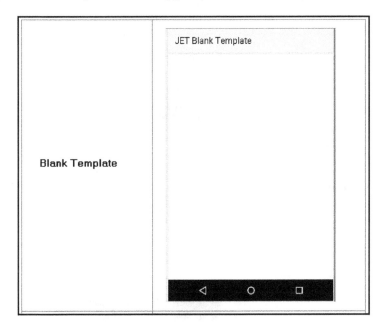

The following screenshot represents the application view created with a navBar template:

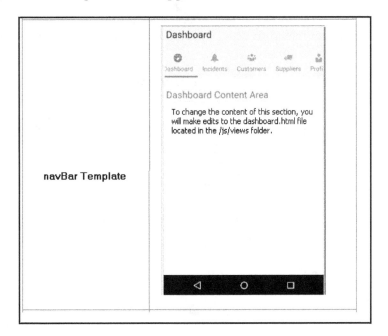

The following screenshot represents the application view created with a navDrawer template:

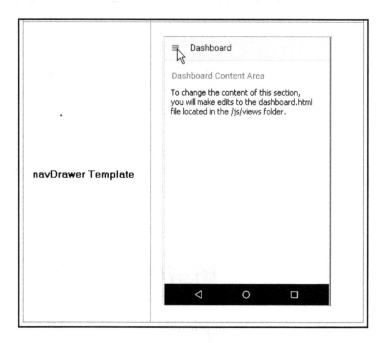

The application created with the above steps contains the folders that include Oracle JET libraries, build scripts, and the application components that can be altered, as per the business requirements of our application.

Some of the important directories and their descriptions are as follows:

Sr.No	Component	Description
1	bower_components	**Contains Bower-managed Oracle JET packages and additional third-party libraries.**
2	hybrid	Contains the application components generated by build and respective platform-specific components.

3	hybrid/config.xml	Contains the Cordova global configuration settings that can be edited to specify core API features, plugins, and platform-specific settings from Cordova.
		For example, the log level (to VERBOSE) on Android and the application orientation (to landscape) can be set using the following setting:
		`<widget id="org.oraclejet.hybridnavbar" version="0.0.1"`
		`xmlns="http://www.w3.org/ns/widgets"xmlns:cdv="http://cordova.apache.org/ns/1.0">`
		`<name>hybrid-navBar</name> ... contents <preference name="LogLevel"`
		`value="VERBOSE"/> <preference name="Orientation" value="landscape" /> </widget>`

4	node_modules	Contains the Node.js modules used by the tooling framework.
5	scripts	Contains Oracle JET build scripts.

Sr.No	Component	Description
6	src	Represents the application Site root, that contains the customizable application components. The content under this application is driven by the choice of template. Irrespective of the template type, index.html and a main.js RequireJS bootstrap component are created. Other templates may contain view templates and viewModel scripts pre-populated with content.

Once the base application is created using the preceding steps, it can be tailored to your business needs by importing it in the standard application editor.

Building and serving the application with Grunt

We can use the Grunt build platform command, as follows, to build our hybrid mobile application with Grunt:

```
grunt build --platform={android|ios} [--buildConfig=path/buildConfig.json]
```

We can use the Grunt serve platform command to launch the hybrid mobile application in a browser, simulator, or mobile device for testing and debugging. The following is the syntax of this command:

```
grunt serve --platform=ios|android [--web=true --serverPort=server-port-
number --livereloadPort=live-reload-port-number --destination=emulator-
name|device --disableLiveReload=true]
```

The additional options for the Grunt serve command are as follows:

Sr.No	Option	Description
1	platform	Desired platform to serve the application. For example, iOS or Android.
2	web	Displays the application in the default web browser if selected as true.
3	serverPort	Server port number to run the application. Defaults to 8000.
4	livereloadPort	Live reload port number for the application. Defaults to 35729.

Sr.No	Option	Description
5	destination	Specifies the name of a preconfigured emulator, such as an **Android Virtual Device** (**AVD**), to run the application. If not specified, the application will be served on the default Android AVD or iOS simulator. We can also serve the application on an actual mobile device, such as iOS, by following the steps advised in the *Packaging and publishing a mobile application* section later.
6	disableLiveReload	Set to true to disable the live reload feature. By setting this option, we can rely on the IDE-specific update serve options.

We can control the serve options to the emulator or web browser, or to the actual device, by running the serve command with diverse options, as follows:

Sr.No	Command	Description
1	grunt serve --platform=android --web=true	Launches the application in the default web browser with the Alta Android theme.
2	grunt serve --platform=ios	Launches the application in the iOS simulator with the Alta iOS theme.
3	grunt serve --platform=android --destination=emulator-name	Launches the application in the specified simulator. The emulator name is case sensitive.
4	grunt serve --platform=android --destination=device	Launches the application in an attached mobile device.

The following is the look and feel of the Oracle JET application across Android, iOS, and Windows themes:

Oracle provides a sample application (*FixItFast*) for live demo, along with installation instructions to configure the same on our system and run it.

> The live demo of the *FixItFast* application is available at `http://www.` `oracle.com/webfolder/technetwork/jet/globalExamples-App-` `FixItFast.html`.

The *FixItFast* sample application includes the introduction, login page, a dashboard view with graphs for statistics, and a list view with clickable images presented across multiple pages. The following are some screenshots from the *FixItFast* demo application:

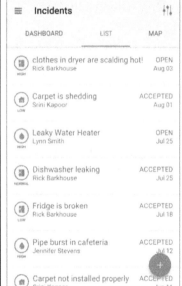

Importing the FixItFast application

The *FixItFast* sample mobile application provided by Oracle JET can be imported to your desktop, and run to review the features and develop your own hybrid mobile application.

Before importing the sample mobile application from *FixItFast*, ensure the `ojet` command-line tool is installed on your desktop as detailed in the following steps:

1. Install Oracle JET cli using the following command:

   ```
   npm -g  install @oracle/ojet-cli
   ```

2. Scaffold the *FixItFast* application from the Oracle template using the following command:

   ```
   ojet create FixItFast --template=
   http://www.oracle.com/webfolder/technetwork/jet
   /public_samples/FixItFast.zip
   ```

3. Running the scaffold command should create the application in the workspace directory, as follows:

```
D:\development\netbeansworkspace>ojet create FixItFast --template=http://www.oracle.com/webfolder/technetwork/jet/public_samples/FixItFast.zip
Oracle JET CLI
Processing template... http://www.oracle.com/webfolder/technetwork/jet/public_samples/FixItFast.zip
Oracle JET: Your app structure is generated. Continuing with library install...
Performing npm install may take a bit...
Invoking npm install
npm WARN prefer global coffee-script@1.10.0 should be installed with -g
FixItFast@1.0.0 D:\development\netbeansworkspace\FixItFast
+-- @oracle/grunt-oraclejet@4.0.0

    +-- ensure-posix-path@1.0.2
    `-- matcher-collection@1.0.5

npm WARN optional SKIPPING OPTIONAL DEPENDENCY: fsevents@~1.0.0 (node_modules\chokidar\node_modules\fsevents):
npm WARN notsup SKIPPING OPTIONAL DEPENDENCY: Unsupported platform for fsevents@1.1.2: wanted {"os":"darwin","arch":"any"} (current: {"os":"win32","arch":"x64"})
Writing  oraclejetconfig.json
Oracle JET: oraclejetconfig.json file exists...checking config...
Oracle JET: Your app is ready! Change to your new app directory FixItFast and try ojet build and serve...

D:\development\netbeansworkspace>
```

4. Open the NetBeans IDE and import the *FixItFast* application by choosing the **File** | **Open Project** wizard as follows:

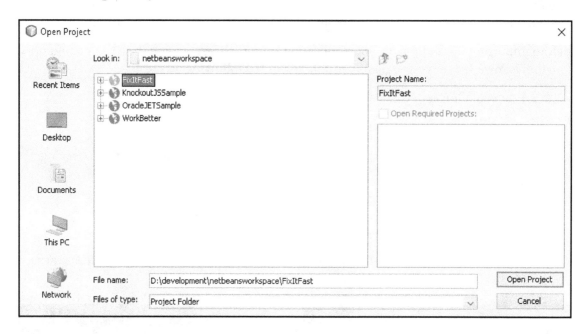

5. The *FixItFast* application can be expanded to observe the folder structure created in the hybrid mobile application we have discussed so far, as follows:

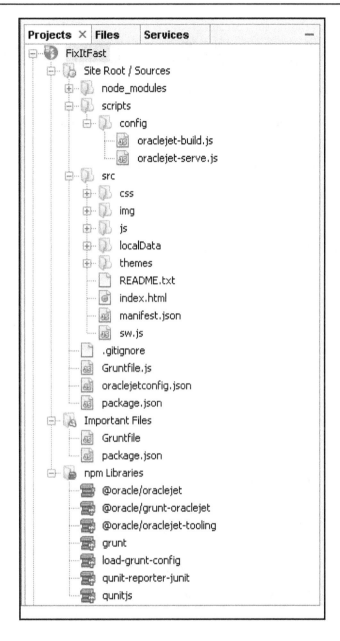

6. We can make the changes we would like to have in this sample application, followed by building and serving the application using Grunt build and serve commands, as discussed previously.

7. Alternatively, we can build and serve from within the NetBeans IDE and test this on our desktop with the device simulator within the Chrome browser (it comes with the Chrome browser, no separate installation required).

The following are the steps to do the same:

1. Right-click on the project and select **Grunt Tasks | build** option, as shown in the following screenshot:

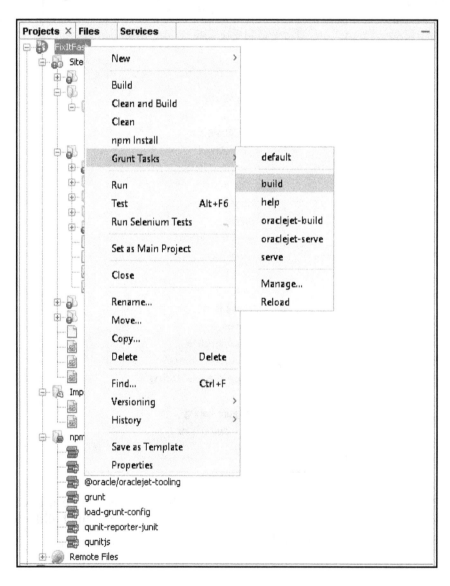

2. The preceding action should trigger a Grunt build on the project and execute the build, as shown in the following screenshot:

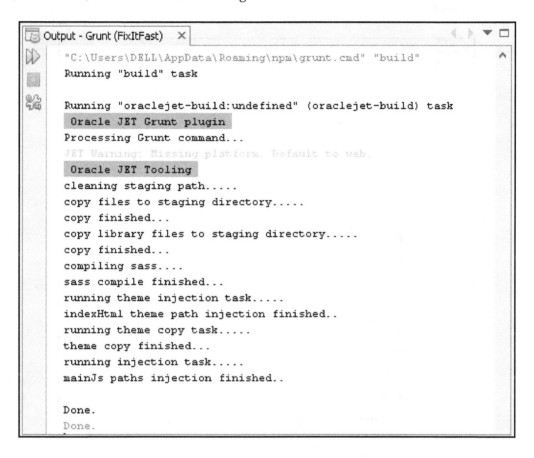

3. Once the grunt build is complete, we can serve the application by right-clicking on the application and selecting **Grunt Tasks** | **serve** as shown in the following screenshot:

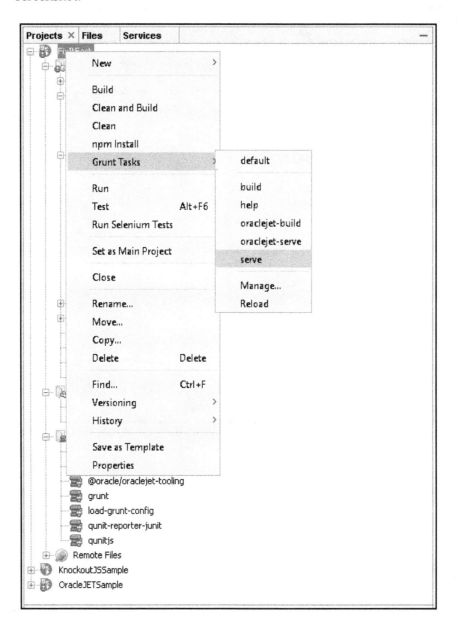

4. The preceding action should execute the Grunt serve on the project, as follows:

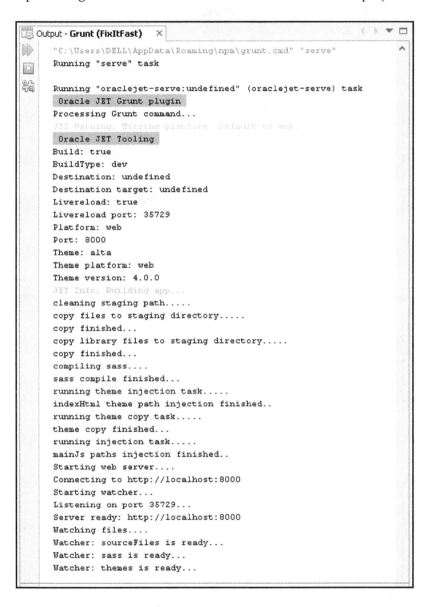

5. Once the preceding step, `grunt - serve`, is executed, it should open the application in the browser as follows. (Remember, you can provide alternate Grunt serve options to run the application on different platforms, as discussed previously.) As I enabled the mobile emulator within the Chrome browser, you can see the following screenshot displaying the page from a mobile perspective:

6. Navigate through the application to review different screens, and play with the device options to see how this application transforms itself based on device, as follows:

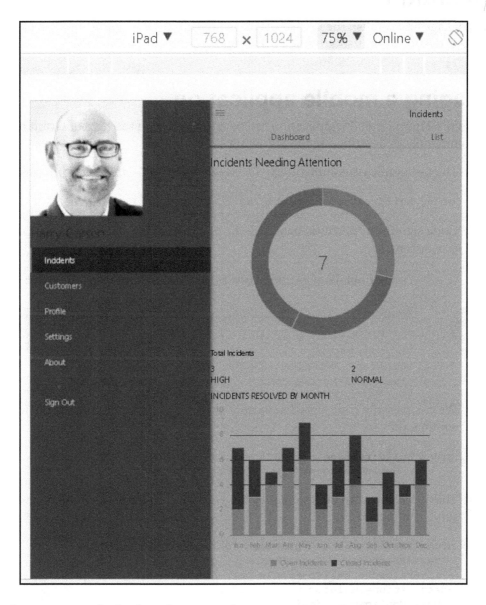

Similarly, you can make further changes to the app or generate your own app to serve as a hybrid mobile app.

Packaging and publishing a mobile application

We can package and publish the Oracle JET-based hybrid mobile applications to Google Play or Apple App stores, using framework support and third-party tools.

Packaging a mobile application

An Oracle JET Hybrid mobile application can be packaged with the help of Grunt build release commands, as described in the following steps:

1. The Grunt release command can be issued with the desired platform as follows:

   ```
   grunt build:release --platform={ios|android}
   ```

2. Code sign the application based on the platform in the `buildConfig.json` component.

   > Further details regarding code sign per platform are available at:
   >
   > **Android:** https://cordova.apache.org/docs/en/latest/guide/platforms/android/tools.html.
   >
   > **iOS:** https://cordova.apache.org/docs/en/latest/guide/platforms/ios/tools.html.

3. We can pass the code sign details and rebuild the application using the following command:

   ```
   grunt build:release --platform={ios|android}
       --buildConfig=path/buildConfig.json
   ```

4. The application can be tested after the preceding changes using the following serve command:

   ```
   grunt serve:release --platform=ios|android [--web=true
   --serverPort=server-port-number
   --livereloadPort=live-reload-port-number -
   -destination=emulator-name|device]
   --buildConfig==path/buildConfig.json
   ```

Publishing a mobile application

Publishing an Oracle JET hybrid mobile application is as per the platform-specific guidelines. Each platform has defined certain standards and procedures to distribute an app on the respective platforms.

Publishing on an iOS platform

The steps involved in publishing iOS applications include:

1. Enrolling in the Apple Developer Program to distribute the app.
2. Adding advanced, integrated services based on the application type.
3. Preparing our application with approval and configuration according to iOS standards.
4. Testing our app on numerous devices and application releases.
5. Submitting and releasing the application as a mobile app in the store. Alternatively, we can also distribute the app outside the store.

The iOS distribution process is represented in the following diagram:

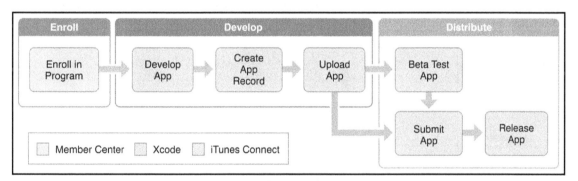

Please note that the process for distributing applications on iOS presented in the preceding diagram is the latest, as of writing this chapter. It may be altered by the iOS team at a later point. The preceding said process is up-to-date, as of writing this chapter.

 For the latest iOS app distribution procedure, please refer to the official iOS documentation at: `https://developer.apple.com/library/ios/ documentation/IDEs/Conceptual/AppDistributionGuide/Introduction/ Introduction.html`.

Publishing on an Android platform

There are multiple approaches to publish our application on Android platforms. The following are the steps involved in publishing the app on Android:

1. Preparing the app for release. We need to perform the following activities to prepare an app for release:
    1. Configuring the app for release, including logs and manifests.
    2. Testing the release version of the app on multiple devices.
    3. Updating the application resources for the release.
    4. Preparing any remote applications or services the app interacts with.
2. Releasing the app to the market through Google Play. We need to perform the following activities to prepare an app for release through Google Play:
    1. Prepare any promotional documentation required for the app.
    2. Configure all the default options and prepare the components.
    3. Publish the prepared release version of the app to Google Play.
3. Alternately, we can publish the application through email, or through our own website, for users to download and install.

The steps involved in publishing Android applications are advised in the following diagram:

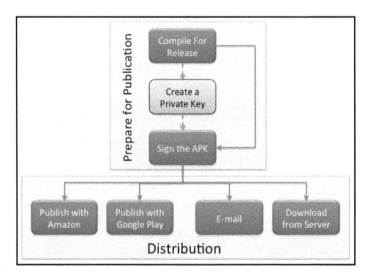

Please note that the process for distributing applications on Android presented in the preceding diagram is the latest, as of writing this chapter. It may be altered by the Android team at a later point.

 For the latest Android app distribution procedure, please refer to the official Android documentation at `http://developer.android.com/ tools/publishing/publishing_overview.html#publishing-release`.

Summary

Throughout this chapter, we learnt the tools required to develop hybrid mobile applications with the Oracle JET framework. We also learnt about developing, building, and serving the hybrid mobile application along with live examples from the Oracle Corporation. We finished this chapter with an understanding of how Oracle JET hybrid mobile applications can be packaged and published to Android-and iOS-based devices in the market.

In the next chapter, we will learn about the essential testing and debugging techniques within the Oracle JET framework in detail.

Testing and Debugging

9

Over the last few decades, software development has seen many radical improvements with the evolution of technology and application development approaches. Agile, test-driven and behavior-driven development methodologies have changed their approach to the application development life cycle from the traditional waterfall model, to deliver working software more rapidly to the end user and to keep adding more features to deliver the expected product in an iterative development method. This change of approach does require the projects to bring automated test regression suites and increase the importance of web application test automation and debugging methods.

In this chapter, we will cover:

- The importance of programmatic testing
- Oracle JET application testing tools
- Debugging Oracle JET applications

The importance of programmatic testing

In the initial days of software development, software testing was considered a phase in the software development life cycle. As software development methodologies are evolving, the importance of including testing in multiple phases of the project has increased. Software testing is the process of finding bugs in the software and making the software bug free. It plays an important role in software development, to assess and expand the quality, reliability, and performance of the product.

Test-driven development (TDD)

Test-driven development (**TDD**) is a progressive approach to software development in which we write the test cases for the target feature, and write just enough production code to fulfill that test scenario and refactor it to meet design principles.

Test-driven development has two levels, namely **Acceptance test-driven development** (**ATDD**) and **Developer test-driven development** (**DTDD**). The following diagram represents the steps involved in this process:

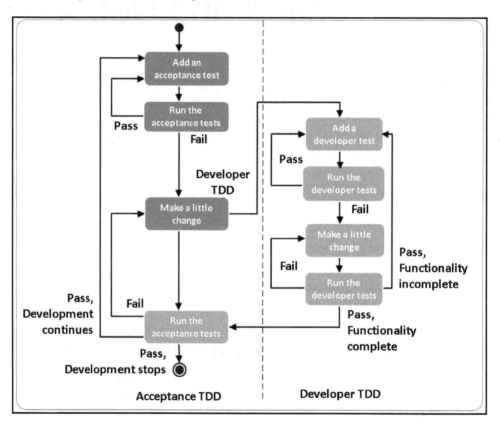

Test-driven development is more successful if we are able to include an automated set of test cases that can be executed each time we run the tests to save the sprint life cycle.

Including a programmatic test case for a client/server-side program makes the development and test life cycle more efficient in terms of automated regression tests, as follows:

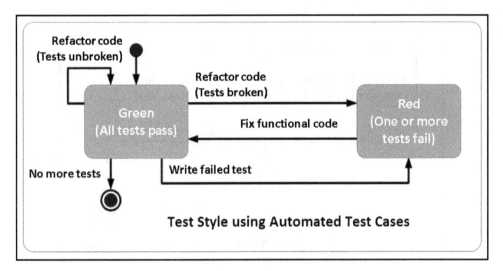

Test Style using Automated Test Cases

The following are the set of characteristics a good unit test should possess:

- Run fast (easy to configure, runtime, and breakdown)
- Run in isolation (with the ability to reorder the test cases)
- Use data that makes unit tests easy to read and to understand
- Use real data (such as production data)
- Represent a phase for the complete functional target

TDD with automated tests also reduces the amount of documentation needed for test performance and improved life cycle.

Agile model-driven development (AMDD)

TDD is not able to envision the bigger design concerns and bind to the overall system design. Such concerns are solved through the AMDD approach; the initial requirements and architecture is envisioned through a spring 0/Iteration 0 cycle. The following is the life cycle representation of the AMDD method:

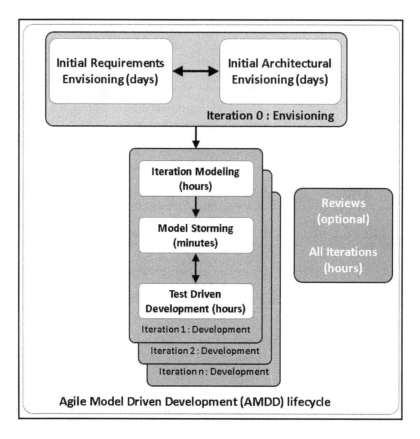

Agile Model Driven Development (AMDD) lifecycle

Behavior-driven development (BDD)

A more refined and business value derived approach for test-driven development is **behavior-driven development (BDD)**, to ensure we are building the right product with no features or tests that don't add business value. The following diagram represents what BDD brings in addition to the TDD approach. It is a more feature-centric development:

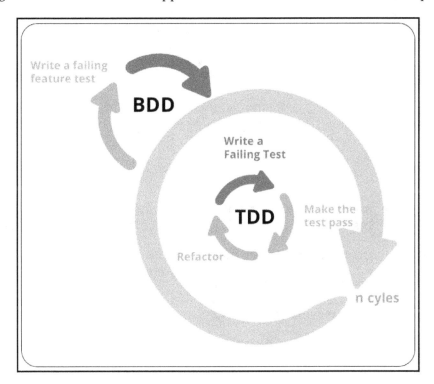

Throughout the natural evolution of testing from TDD and AMDD to BDD, the need for the regression testing of software components as we keep upgrading features has increased. This regression testing will consume more time and budget if handled manually. Hence, the need for automated regression tests by delivering iterative development includes solving more detailed user stories as we go through a number of sprints. It is highly recommended that you have automated/programmatic test cases for the software to ensure the functionality delivered by previous sprints (or development cycles) is quickly retested, while adding new functionality to the software components.

Oracle JET application testing tools

Before reviewing the set of tools that will help us programmatically test/unit test applications developed with Oracle JET, let us understand a unit that is eligible for unit testing. In an ideal scenario, a unit is an independent function that repeatedly produces the same result for a set of input parameters. It is a good idea to start unit tests before dealing with complex scenarios, including DOM manipulation. It has been observed that building unit test cases is easier if you are doing it while you are developing each unit of function with the knowledge of the purpose of that function. However, we can write unit test cases that cover most of our code and uncover potential bugs that may not have been tested before.

Applications developed with Oracle JET can be programmatically tested with any of the following web applications/JavaScript testing tools.

QUnit

QUnit is one of the prevailing JavaScript unit test frameworks being used by leading software developments including Oracle JET, jQuery, jQuery UI, and mobile projects.

It can be installed using either of the following commands:

- For NPM, use the following command:

```
npm install --save-dev qunitjs
```

- For YARN, use the following command:

```
yarn add qunitjs --dev
```

- For Bower, use the following command:

```
bower install --save-dev qunit
```

Let us review a simple example of QUnit now and see how it executes the JavaScript unit test cases on pages.

Once we install QUnit in our project, we can write the following web content to invoke QUnit test cases:

```
//HTML:

<div id="qunit"></div>
<div id="qunit-fixture"></div>

//JavaScript:

var data = {
  ControlPanel: {
    CurrentInOrder: 1
  },
  Questions: [{
    Text: "Human Capital Management"
  }, {
    Text: "Payroll"
  }, {
    Text: "Benefits"
  }, {
    Text: "Financials"
  }]
};

test("A very simple test of no value", function () {
  ok(1 == "1", "Test passed! (But we didn't test anything)");
});

test("Array should contain four items", function () {
  equal(data.Questions.length, 4, "Pass! - array contains four items");
});

test("Does Array contain five items?", function () {
  equal(data.Questions.length, 5, "Fail! - array does not contain five
items");
});
```

Once the preceding code snippets are added to the web components, running the application should open this page with the QUnit test cases executed as follows:

QUnit Unit Test Case

Hide passed tests Check for Globals No try-catch

Mozilla/5.0 (Windows NT 10.0; Win64; x64) AppleWebKit/537.36 (KHTML, like Gecko) Chrome/61.0.3163.100 Safari/537.36

Tests completed in 21 milliseconds
2 assertions of 3 passed, 1 failed.

1. A very simple test of no value (0, 1, 1)   1 ms

  1. Test passed! (But we didn't test anything)

2. Array should contain four items (0, 1, 1)   0 ms

  1. Pass! - array contains four items

3. Does Array contain five items? (1, 0, 1)   Rerun   2 ms

  1. Fail! - array does not contain five items
  Expected: 5
    Result: 4
      Diff: 5 4
    Source: at Object.<anonymous> (http://fiddle.jshell.net/_display/:52:5)

From the preceding test case, you can observe that out of three test cases, two of them passed, and all the test case results are highlighted on the QUnit result page. You can also customize the result using the **Hide passed tests**, **Check for Globals**, and **No try-catch** options.

Oracle JET components seamlessly integrate with the QUnit for unit testing web page components.

 More details about the QUnit framework are available at its home page: https://qunitjs.com/.

Jasmine

Jasmine is an independent unit testing framework for effectively testing JavaScript components in a behavior-driven development architecture.

It can be added to our environment using the following commands:

1. Install using Node.js as follows:

```
npm install --save-dev jasmine
```

2. Initialize Jasmine for our project:

```
./node_modules/.bin/jasmine init
```

Once Jasmine is installed, we can add the following web content to the components to unit test the respective components:

- HTML:

```
//no additional content required
```

- JavaScript:

```
var ourDataArray = {
  ControlPanel: {
  CurrentInOrder: 1
  },
  Questions: [{
    Text: "Human Capital Management"
  }, {
    Text: "Payroll"
  }, {
    Text: "Benefits"
  }, {
    Text: "Financials"
  }]
};
describe("Our data array", function() {
  it("has four items?", function() {
    expect(ourDataArray.Questions.length).toBe(4);
  });
});
describe("Our data array", function() {
  it("has five items?", function() {
    expect(ourDataArray.Questions.length).toBe(5);
  });
});
describe("Our data array", function() {
  it("has two properties?", function() {
    expect(Object.keys(ourDataArray).length).toBe(2);
  });
});
```

Once the preceding code snippets are added to the web components, running the application should open this page, with the Jasmine test cases executed as follows:

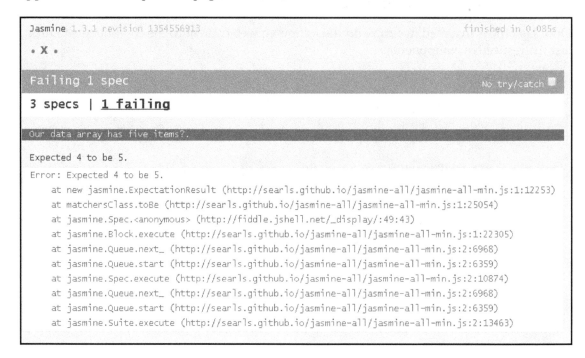

In the preceding result, we can see **1 failing** test case, however we can click on the **3 specs** link to see the overall status of the unit test cases as well:

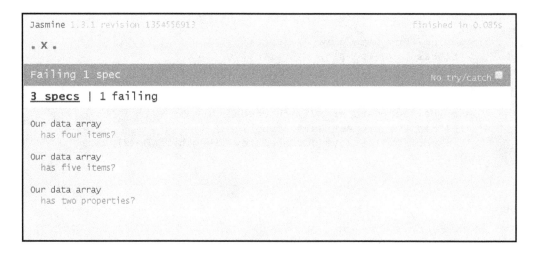

The green dots above the status header represent the pass unit test cases, while the cross marks represent the fail unit test cases.

We can test Oracle JET components with the Jasmine framework, by accessing the objects using JavaScript and testing the assertions throughout the test case.

> As per `https://jasmine.github.io/setup/nodejs.html`, you must customize `spec`, `support`, and `jasmine.json` to enumerate the source files and spec files you would like the Jasmine runner to include. More details about the Jasmine framework are available at its home page: `https://jasmine.github.io/`.

Mocha

Mocha is an asynchronous JavaScript testing framework that runs on Node.js and has salient features to support unit testing the web components.

We can install Mocha globally with `npm` using the following command:

```
npm install --global mocha
```

We can install it as a development dependency to our project using the following command:

```
npm install --save-dev mocha
```

We can also use `chai`, an easy to consume behavior/test-driven development assertion library for JavaScript testing frameworks. We use the following command:

```
npm install chai
```

Once Mocha and Chai are installed, we can add the following web content to the components to unit test the respective components:

```
//HTML

<div id="mocha"></div>

//JavaScript

var ourDataArray = {
  Questions: [{
    Text: "Human Capital Management"
  }, {
    Text: "Payroll"
```

```
  }, {
    Text: "Benefits"
  }, {
    Text: "Financials"
  }]
};
mocha.setup('bdd');
var expect = chai.expect;
describe('Matching Numbers', function() {
  it('Matching zero as a number', function() {
    expect(0).to.equal(0);
  });
});
describe('Array Length matching', function() {
  it('has four items?', function() {
    expect(ourDataArray.Questions.length).to.equal(4);
  });
});
describe('Array Length assertion', function() {
  it('has five items?', function() {
    expect(ourDataArray.Questions.length).to.equal(5);
  });
});
mocha.run();
```

Once the preceding code snippets are added to the web components, running the application should open this page, with the Mocha test cases executed as follows:

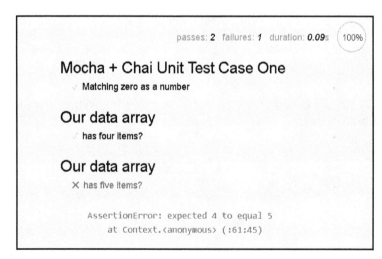

In the preceding result, we can see the first two unit test cases are passing while the third one is failing, along with the failure description.

We can test Oracle JET components with the Mocha and Chai frameworks by accessing the objects using JavaScript and testing the assertions throughout the test case. Also note that Mocha has the power to test asynchronous code.

One of the powerful features of Mocha and Chai is hooks. With its default BDD-style interface, Mocha provides the hooks `before()`, `after()`, `beforeEach()`, and `afterEach()`. These can be used to set up preconditions and clean up after your tests.

> More details about the Mocha and Chai frameworks are available at their home pages:
>
> Mocha: `https://mochajs.org/`.
> Chai: `http://chaijs.com/`.

Jest, Cucumber, Enzyme, Tape, and AVA are the other trending JavaScript test frameworks with salient features.

AVA is a multithreaded JavaScript testing framework that runs on Node.js for the purposes of IO intense unit testing for web components. It provides three times improved test execution performance compared to the Mocha framework. It lets us write more atomic test cases which benefits concurrent test execution abilities.

> More details about these frameworks, along with examples, are available at the following URLs:
>
> AVA: `https://github.com/avajs/ava`.
> Jest: `https://facebook.github.io/jest/`.
> Cucumber: `https://cucumber.io/`.
> Enzyme: `https://github.com/airbnb/enzyme`.
> Tape: `https://github.com/substack/tape`.

Selenium WebDriver

This is an alternative approach to test the web application developed with Oracle JET with the help of WebDriver components from the Selenium test suite.

Selenium is famous for building automated test suites for web interfaces by detecting the UI components and writing test cases with sets of requests and response assertions.

With the inclusion of a WebDriver in Selenium and the advent of browser-based support, Selenium is now more powerful and lets us automate UI component testing. The Selenium WebDriver makes direct calls to the browser using each browser's native support for automation.

It can be added to a Node.js environment using the following command:

```
npm install selenium-webdriver
```

More details about the Selenium WebDriver, along with install instructions and examples, are available at: `http://www.seleniumhq.org/projects/webdriver/`.

Running JavaScript unit tests

Once we develop the web interfaces along with unit test cases, as advised in the preceding sections, we can run them using different approaches. One of the more developer-friendly approaches is to use the test runners within the IDE.

While there are number of plugins to help us with this requirement, the Karma and JS Test Driver test runners are the most prominent unit test run tools from IDE. Let us review both the tools and understand how they help with unit tests run from IDE.

Karma

Karma makes unit testing instantaneous and simple for developers, as it does not have any heavy configurations or load any external dependencies. In addition, it gives more control to the developer with support for the testing of real devices, remote workflow tests, debugging, and continuous integration support.

We can install Karma in our project using the following command:

```
npm install karma --save-dev
```

We can also install Karma along with the Jasmine unit test support using the following command:

```
npm install karma-jasmine karma-chrome-launcher jasmine-core --save-dev
```

We can also install the command-line interface if we want to avoid starting the program with the node modules command. We use the following install command:

```
npm install -g karma-cli
```

Once Karma is installed in the development environment, we can configure it for our project in NetBeans IDE by completing the following steps:

1. Create a skeleton Karma configuration file using the **File** | **New File** option as follows:

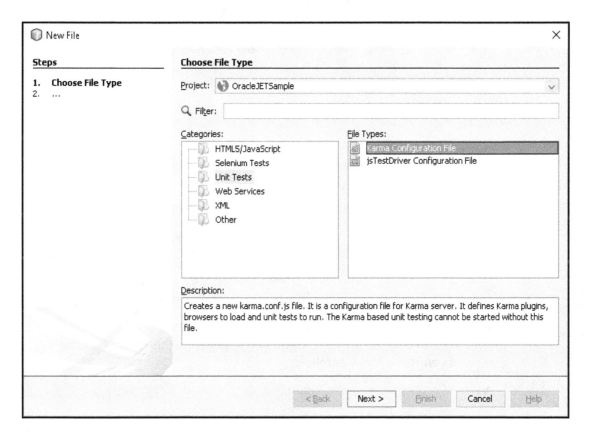

2. Select unit tests as the **Karma Configuration File** and click **Next>** to let the IDE provide the new configuration file wizard, as follows:

3. Click **Finish** to let it generate the `karma.conf.js` Karma config file in the project. We can also use the `init` command to generate this config file. The generated config file looks as follows:

```
 karma.conf.js ×

Source  History      🔄 🖼 ▾ 🖼 ▾ 🔍 🔁 🔁 🖼 🗔 🔁 🔁 🔁 🔁 🔁 ⏺ ▣ 🔁 ▰

  1  ☐  /*
  2     * To change this license header, choose License Headers in Project ↵
        Properties.
  3     * To change this template file, choose Tools | Templates
  4     * and open the template in the editor.
  5     */
  6
  7     module.exports = function (config) {
  8         config.set({
  9             basePath: '../',
 10
 11             files: [
 12             ],
 13
 14             exclude: [
 15             ],
 16
 17             autoWatch: true,
 18
 19             frameworks: [
 20             ],
 21
 22             browsers: [
 23             ],
 24
 25             plugins: [
 26             ]
 27         });
 28     };
 29
```

4. We can add all the required dependencies and configurations to this file.

Additional documentation about Karma configuration is available
at `http://karma-runner.github.io/1.0/config/configuration-file.html`.

5. Right-click on the project and select **Properties | JavaScript Testing**. Then set the **Testing Provider** as **Karma** and browse for `karma.conf.js` in the project root folder as follows:

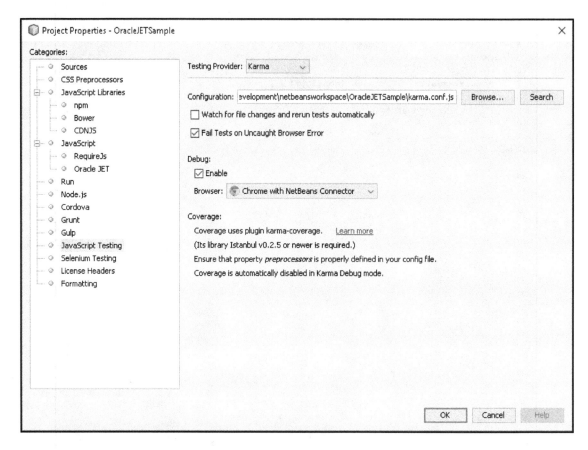

6. This will generate a new option in the project root as **Karma**, as follows:

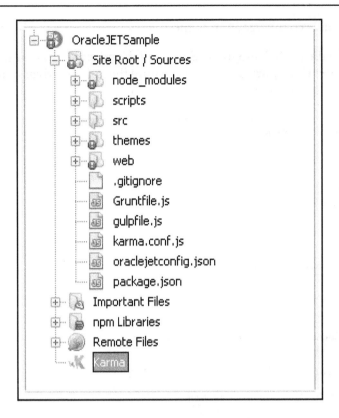

7. Right click on **Karma** and start to run the test engine. It will start the Karma test engine within a web interface. Once Karma is started, we can right-click on the project and select **Test** to run the unit test cases on the project.

JS test driver

An alternate approach to using Karma for running unit tests from JavaScript web projects (whether developed with Oracle JET or not) is to use JS test driver.

It is available for installation under the downloads section at `http://code.google.com/p/js-test-driver/`.

Once the installation is completed, follow these steps to use JS Test Driver:

1. In the NetBeans IDE, go to the **Services** tab and right-click on **JS Test Driver**. Choose the **Configure** option to configure the JS Test Driver as shown in the following screenshot:

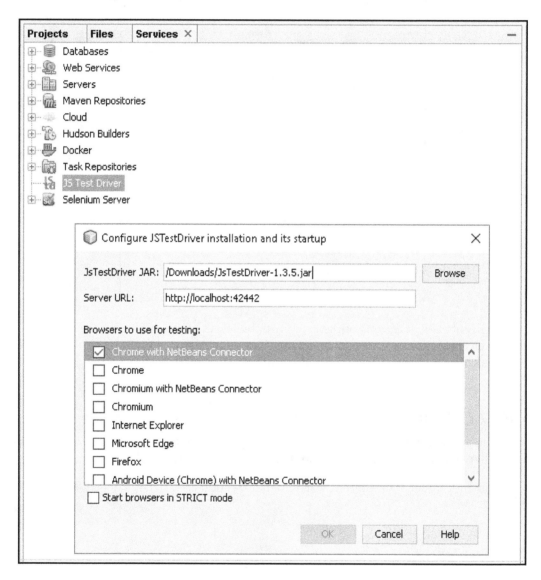

2. Once the test driver is configured, generate the JS Test Runner init configuration file by right-clicking on the project and selecting the **New File**, **Unit Tests**, and **JSTestDriver Configuration File** options, as shown in the following screenshot:

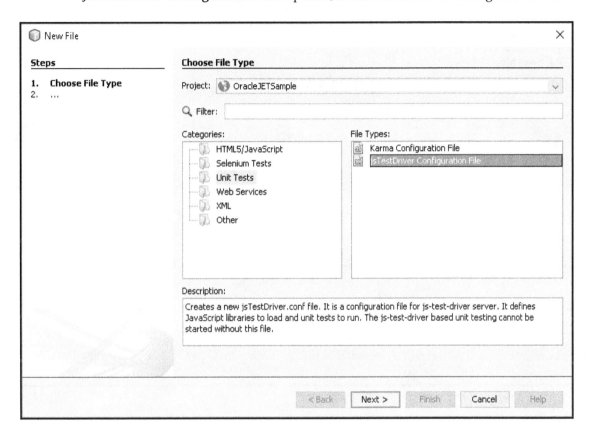

3. Click on **Next>** to let the `jsTestDriver.conf.js` file wizard open as follows:

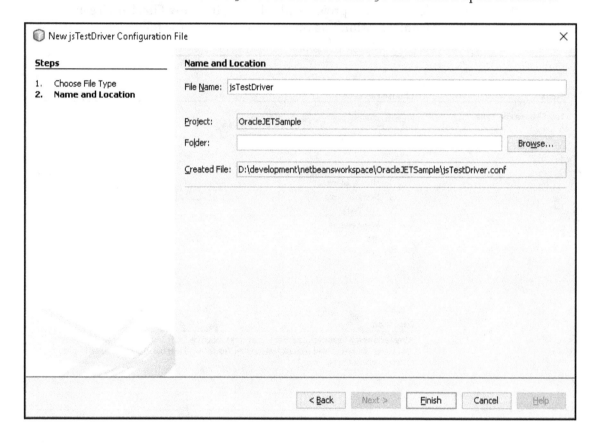

4. Click on **Finish** to create the configuration file. We can add the configurations to the `jsTestDriver.conf.js` file, including JasmineAdapter, framework dependencies, and the `/unit/tests/*.js` unit test directory reference.

5. Once the configuration is completed, right-click on the project and select **Test** to let the **JS test runner** start and open the web interface in the browser. We can select the **Test Results perspective from windows** | **Output** options on the IDE.

Also, Oracle recommends using the `oj.BusyContext` API in automated testing.

The various test tools covered in this section can be used to test the application, which has various components—Collections, Controls, Forms, Frameworks (Binding, Router, Switcher), Layout, and Navigation—of the Oracle JET framework.

Debugging Oracle JET applications

Debugging the web interface application is a bit tricky, especially when dealing with JavaScript-based content. With a number of components being reused and developed by multiple developers across the project, managing the dependencies across multiple production releases and reviewing any defects that are raised in web interface components, is a tricky exercise.

Using browser extensions

One option is to review the output by inserting console output and checking the browser console. (For example, select **More Tools** | **Developer Tools** from Chrome's main menu. Right-click a page element and select **Inspect**.) Developer tools have features such as device mode, elements panel, console, sources, network, performance, memory, application, and security panels to help us debug the application further.

The following is a screenshot of the Oracle JET page with browser debugging enabled and populating the components loading through the network:

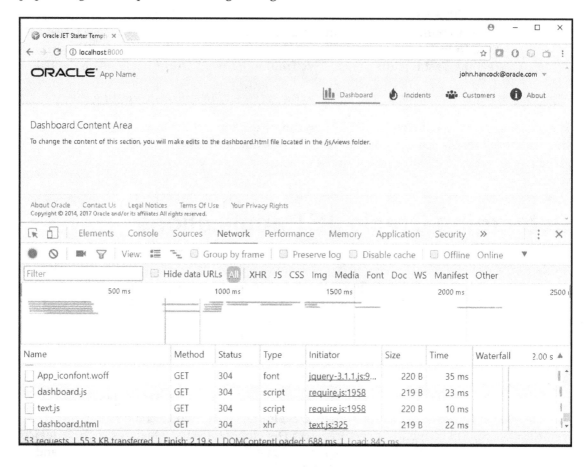

Using IDE extensions

We can also use the IDE JS Test Driver debug option by setting the break points in the project and running the tests. To evaluate any specific expression, we can choose the **Debug | Evaluate Expression** option so that expression value is shown from a debugging perspective.

Debugging an Oracle JET hybrid (mobile) application involves diverse approaches on a browser, emulator, and on an actual device. We can serve the application with the platform attribute specified to debug on the respective platform.

Summary

Throughout this chapter, we learnt the importance of the programmatic testing of web applications and gained a deep understanding of changing project development life cycles. We also learnt about the tools and techniques for unit testing applications developed in JavaScript and Oracle JET. We finished this chapter with an understanding of how to run the unit tests from within IDE, and how to debug Oracle JET-based web applications.

In the next chapter, we will learn about essential version migration and the future of the Oracle JET framework in detail.

10
Security and Version Migration

Application vulnerabilities and security breaches are growing with newer methods of application development. A rich application doesn't just mean having rich functional features or a fancy user interface, but also involves protection from the risks of modern application hacking techniques. It is important for developers to be aware of common application vulnerabilities and how to program well to protect applications from such attacks. Also, it is important to safely and securely migrate our applications to newer versions of the framework to adopt the security updates offered by the software upgrade.

In this chapter, we will cover:

- Common web application vulnerabilities
- Oracle JET security offerings
- Version migration with Oracle JET
- The future of the Oracle JET framework

Common web application vulnerabilities

Application developers should be aware of the security guidelines and follow the standards to ensure they build a secure web application. Web application vulnerabilities are some of the commonly occurring mistakes in application development, and can lead to data breach in our applications and can compromise our applications' security. There are a number of software solutions (such as CheckMarx) available to determine security violations in applications via a software scan, and to fix the problems. Let us review the most common web application vulnerabilities in the upcoming sections.

Cross-Site Scripting (XSS)

An XSS vulnerability occurs due to insufficient client-side validation on web pages if the web pages load the data from users and include this in web pages without validating the data. This lets the hacker's script execute on a victim's browser and show arbitrary content, that the victim believes is real and from the application, and so he provides his information. This means that XSS attacks potentially harm the users of the application (victims) but not the application itself. The following diagram represents the flow of a **Cross-Site Scripting (XSS)** attack:

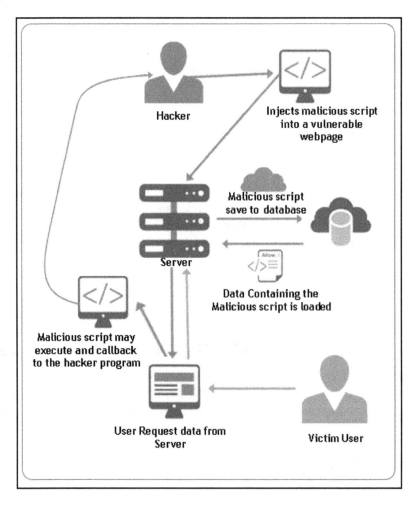

XSS vulnerability attacks are powerful, as they execute directly in the victim's session rather than on the server. Hence, they should be restricted in the initial stages, during which scripts from users are allowed and included in web pages.

There are different types of XSS attacks, including Reflective XSS (false emails sent with links containing malicious scripts) and Persistent XSS (web applications that store user information in local browser databases). The following are the consequences of XSS vulnerabilities:

- Hijacking the user account in the targeted web application
- Web worms injection
- Reading the user clipboard and browser history to read secure information
- Remotely controlling the user session or browsers
- Compromising intranet security and data

XSS attacks can be restricted by doing the following:

- Validating the user input to the web application with both client-side and server-side validations
- Encoding both request and response content to the web application

SQL injection

SQL queries are the most common way of storing and accessing information in web applications. SQL injection is a way of introducing the database queries into the application's user interface form fields and accessing the entire application information, including other users' details. SQL injection occurs if the application fails to sanitize the untrusted data and run the SQL queries with it. The attackers use specially crafted SQL queries injected through form fields and access the application details from the database.

With SQL injection, the application attackers can do the following:

- Control the application data and change the system behavior
- Alter the application data without having the right access permissions, for example alter your bank balance by accessing your bank account
- Compromise client data and degrade the application performance by running long running queries

SQL injection attacks can be controlled by doing the following:

- Using parameterized queries and prepared statements between the application and database
- Restricting the usage of special characters that can be used as part of SQL injection
- Giving the minimum amount of privileges from the application's users to the database

LDAP injection

LDAP injection is another type of attack on application users and involves placing suspicious code in a victim user's application form fields and gaining unauthorized access. Once the hacker gets access to the application using this approach, they can access the application on their own and compromise user information.

Web applications should thoroughly sanitize the users' input data before using **Lightweight Directory Access Protocol (LDAP)** statements.

LDAP injection can compromise application credentials, security, financial status, and organization reputation.

LDAP injection can be controlled by periodically changing the credentials, binding the user access to their location and systems, using one-time passwords and random key generation devices secured with passwords, asking for random user information, and controlling multiple-session usage for the same account.

CRLF injection

CRLF refers to the special character blocks **carriage return and line feed**. They are embedded as part of HTTP headers, MIME (emails), and NNTP (news groups) to help split text streams into discrete elements. Attackers use specifically designed words with CRLF injections that can confuse the web application by executing harmful commands in a vulnerable component of the application.

CRLF injection can lead to serious security threats including XSS, proxy, and cache spoil, and can hijack an active user session or control the client's web browsers.

CRLF injection attacks can be controlled by thoroughly validating the user's input and ensuring the encoding is applied on request and response by including HTTP headers to the request/response.

Cross-Site Request Forgery (CSRF)

Cross-Site Request Forgery (**CSRF**) attacks occur through a malicious website that sends the requests to the targeted application website if the user is already authenticated through a different website. These attacks happen if the user logs in to the actual website and leaves the session open, and accesses the malicious website links and forms that try to form the dynamic URLs to the targeted application where the user has already logged in.

The best way to prevent CSRF attacks is to attach CSRF tokens to each request from the application users and bind them to the user session. This way, the applications can restrict the access to the user's secure information by confirming the request is coming from known user sessions.

Insecure cryptographic storage

Insecure cryptographic storage is a vulnerability in that secure information in an application is not securely stored. This lets attackers access the secure information, including accessing other applications or datastores and compromising system security.

These vulnerabilities can be avoided by ensuring the secure data is encrypted, maintaining proper key storage, erasing sensitive datastores when they are no longer required by the application, using rich application algorithms, and following standard cryptography techniques.

Buffer overflow

A buffer is a consecutive segment in the system memory which is assigned to the application to store information based on the data type. A buffer overflow or overrun occurs when the application buffer is not properly managed by the program and assigns more data than the buffer can handle. The result of this is buffer corruption or allowing the attackers access to the buffer.

Buffer overflow attacks can be controlled by following coding standards and clearing the variable values and objects within the program after their usage. Running buffer cleanup programs on a scheduled basis also helps in restricting this vulnerability and improving application performance.

Directory traversal

Directory traversal is an HTTP adventure program through which hackers get unauthorized system access and read restricted files and directories.

The applications usually follow either of the root directory access or **access control lists (ACLs)** methods, and give restricted access to the application files and directories for any user. Directory traversal occurs by letting the user input be submitted to the program without thoroughly validating it.

Applications should engage user input validation, restrict special characters, and avoid characters that are commonly used by hackers to access application directories. It is also advisable to update the applications and servers with the latest software, patches, and framework upgrades to ensure a more secure application is employed.

Other security vulnerabilities include failure to restrict URL access, insufficient transport layer protection, and malicious code.

Oracle JET security offerings

Oracle JET applications support all common web application security standards and best practices, including the **Open Web Application Security Project (OWASP)**, the **Web Application Security Project (WASP)**, and the **Web Application Security Working Group (WASWG)**. In addition to this, the Oracle JET framework provides authorization for user-specific data access with the `oj.OAuth` plugin.

The Oracle JET framework has also developed secure coding standards that mitigate security threats, including:

- Strict mode of execution for all JavaScript components
- No inline script elements are adopted for framework components
- No random number generation logic is employed

The Oracle JET motivates us to include mechanisms for sanitizing strings via established guidelines for dealing with XSS attacks in our own code and content.

Oracle JET framework offers the `oj.OAuth` plugin, which supports the OAuth 2.0 standards. It is a standard mechanism to provide access to users without having to review their login credentials. The following are the roles defined by OAuth 2.0:

- **Resource owner**: The component that holds the power to grant access for any user to a protected resource
- **Client**: The application that requests access to the protected resources
- **Resource server**: The server that accepts requests with access tokens and supplies protected resource access
- **Authorization server**: The server that authenticates the resource owner and provides access tokens to the client for secure resource access

The following flowchart represents the sequence of steps happening in OAuth authorization:

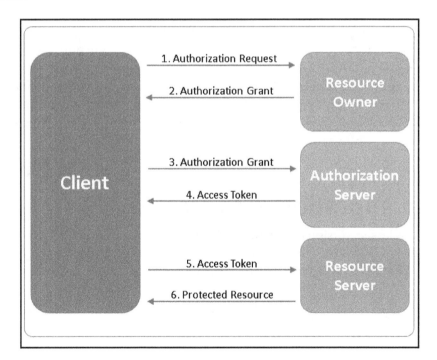

The following are the steps involved in enabling OAuth2.0 authorization in our application:

1. **Initialize the oj.OAuth object**: We can initialize the `oj.OAuth` object using the following code:

   ```
   var myOAuth = new OAuth(header, attributes);
   ```

   `header` is the MIME header and the `attributes` can be `client_id`, `client_secret`, `bearer_url`, and any additional attributes.

2. **Verify the oj.OAuth object initialization**: The `oj.OAuth` object created from the preceding step can be verified using the following code:

   ```
   var initFlag = myOAuth.isInitialized();
   ```

3. **Obtain the OAuth header**: The `oj.OAuth` header can be accessed using the following code:

   ```
   var myHeaders = myOAuth.getHeader();
   ```

4. **Use oj.OAuth with the Oracle JET Common model**: `oj.OAuth` can be added to the view model using either embedded or external plugin approaches.
5. **Integrate oj.OAuth with Oracle Identity Management (iDM)**: `oj.OAuth` can be integrated with the Oracle iDM server using two levels of authorization:
   - Keeping client credentials on the application proxy server.
   - The iDM servers need a `access_token` authorization header which is a non-standard version.

Version migration with Oracle JET

Oracle JET has released version 4.0.0 with the DOM syntax for defining all JET UI components in an HTML page, including the `@oracle/ojet-cli` Oracle JET command-line interface. This means that the usage of Yeoman and Grunt builds are optional now.

However, upgrading an existing JET application to v4.0.0 does not require you to move to the new custom element syntax.

If you are using an older version of Oracle JET already (v2.1.0, v2.2.0, v2.3.0, or v3.2.0), it is very easy to migrate to the latest version (v4.0.0). While Bower and Git tooling dependencies are discounted in the v3.x.x upgrade, Yeoman and Grunt builds were made optional with the `ojet-cli` being introduced in v.4.0.0. Please follow the following step-by-step procedure to safely migrate your application to the latest version (v4.0.0):

1. Clean the npm cache using the following command:

```
npm cache clean
```

2. Upgrade the generator-Oracle JET to use the latest version tooling using the following command:

```
[sudo] npm uninstall -g generator-oraclejet
[sudo] npm install -g @oracle/ojet-cli
```

3. Upgrade the local npm dependencies from the application root directory as follows:

```
cd appDir
npm uninstall oraclejet grunt-oraclejet oraclejet-tooling
npm install @oracle/oraclejet @oracle/oraclejet-tooling --save
```

4. Import the latest theme and configure it to include your custom theme with the following command:

```
@import "../../../../node_modules/oraclejet/dist/scss
        /alta-android/oj-alta";
```

5. Replace your application's HTML page CSS entries with the following, latest version of the Alta UI CSS entry:

```
<link rel="stylesheet" href="css/libs/oj/v4.0.0/alta/oj-alta-
min.css" id="css" />
```

6. Update the Oracle library entries and jQuery dependencies to the latest versions.
7. If your application has any custom Bower, Grunt, or Yeoman components, you can continue using them. Otherwise, you can remove them using the following commands:

```
[sudo] npm uninstall bower -g
[sudo] npm uninstall -g yo
[sudo] npm uninstall -g grunt-cli
```

8. Build and serve the application to see it working on the latest version.

The preceding steps are for the standard version migration if you have strictly used Oracle JET components. For those adding custom components and external libraries, please make the relevant changes to avoid any impact on the functionality of the version migration.

The future of the Oracle JET framework

Oracle JET, being the standard web and hybrid application development framework from the Oracle Corporation, is the obvious choice for applications that are already using Oracle products and middleware. Being an open source framework and adhering to open web standards, it has a great reputation in the market due to its rich, technical backing from the Oracle Corporation.

While Oracle JET v4.0.0 introduced a new DOM syntax for defining all JET UI components in HTML, making all JET UI components custom components for intuitive access remains close to the HTML5 specification.

As specified in the previous section, for migrating our existing JET application to v4.0.0, we don't have to move to the new custom element syntax. But if you are starting development of new applications on v4.0.0, it is highly recommended that you start with the custom element syntax.

Oracle JET is planning to stop data-bind syntax support (supported in older versions of 3.x.x. and below) after the upcoming release of v8.0.0 (planned to release approximately two years from the v4.0.0 release).

Summary

Throughout this chapter, we learnt about common web application vulnerabilities and Oracle JET support for building a secure web application. We also learnt about version migration to the latest Oracle JET version (4.0.0) from older versions and looked at an overview of the newly added features. We finished this chapter with an understanding of the future of the Oracle JET framework, along with planned releases.

For more information about Oracle JET, the best source of information I would recommend is the official Oracle documentation at `http://www.oracle.com/webfolder/technetwork/jet/index.html`.

We are anticipating that the Oracle JET framework will be updated with more interesting features in upcoming versions. We will get back to you with the next version of this book, along with Oracle JET updates to help you learn the new features in updated versions. Happy coding!

Index

directory traversal 256

E

external data access 94

F

form components
  about 101
  selection components 111
  text input components 101
form controls 123, 126
form page style 42

G

gauges
  about 137
  dial gauges 138
  LED gauges 139
  rating gauges 141
  status meter gauges 143
Grunt 50
  about 48
  installing 15
Gulp
  about 52
  automation 52
  installing 52, 53, 55
  platform-agnostic 52
  simple 52
  strong ecosystem 52

H

Hybrid mobile application development
  about 203, 204, 205, 206
  Android platform, publishing 222, 223
  building, with Grunt 207, 209
  FixItFast application, importing 211, 212, 214,
    215, 216, 217, 218, 219
  iOS platform, publishing 221
  packaging 220
  publishing 220, 221
  serving, with Grunt 207, 209

I

IDE extensions
  using 248
insecure cryptographic storage 255
Integrated Development Environment (IDE) 23
interactive bindings 93
internationalization 189

J

Jasmine
  about 232, 233, 234, 235
  reference link 235
JavaScript Extension Toolkit (JET) 8
JavaScript optimization techniques 188
JavaScript unit tests
  executing 238
  JS test driver 243, 244, 245, 246, 247
  Karma 238, 239, 240, 242
JS test runner 247

K

Knockout.js
  about 66
  automatic view refresh 67
  declarative bindings 67
  dependency management 67
  extensibility 67
  features 67
  installation 68, 70, 73, 75, 76
  language 67
  programming 68, 70, 73, 75, 76
  UI template 67
  utilities 67

L

layout components
  about 150
  example 151
LDAP injection 254
LESS (Leaner CSS) 48
Lightweight Directory Access Protocol (LDAP) 254
localization 189

P

performance
  about 188
  CSS optimization techniques 188
  JavaScript optimization techniques 188
  Oracle JET component optimization techniques 189
programmatic testing
  about 225
  agile model-driven development (AMDD) 228
  behavior-driven development (BDD) 229
  test-driven development (TDD) 226, 227

Q

QUnit
  about 230, 231, 232
  URL 232

R

recommendations 45
RequireJS
  about 56
  installing 57, 60
  URL, for downloading 57
responsiveness
  about 183, 186
  media queries 186

S

selection components
  about 111
  check box set 116
  combo box 114
  radio set 119
  select 111
  switch 122
Selenium WebDriver
  about 237, 238
  reference link 238
Single-Page Application (SPA) 9, 166
SQL injection 253, 254
Syntactically Awesome StyleSheets (Sass) 48

T

test-driven development (TDD)
  about 226, 227
  Acceptance test-driven development (ATDD) 226
  Developer test-driven development (DTDD) 226
text input components
  about 101
  input date 106
  input date time 109
  input number 105
  input password 102
  input text 101
  input time 108
  text area 103
Theme Builder
  references 193

V

validations
  about 169
  application level validations 173, 179, 180
  component validations 169, 173
  converters 180, 182
version migration
  with Oracle JET 258, 259, 260
visualization components
  about 133
  charts 134
  gauges 137
  sunbursts 146
  type 145

W

WAI-ARIA (Web Accessibility Initiative-Accessible Rich Internet Applications) 190
Web Application Security Project (WASP) 256
Web Application Security Working Group (WASWG) 256
webpack
  about 61
  reference link 63
wizards 42, 44

www.ingramcontent.com/pod-product-compliance
Lightning Source LLC
Chambersburg PA
CBHW080631060326
40690CB00021B/4893